Practical Data Science for Information Professionals

Every purchase of a Facet book helps to fund CILIP's advocacy, awareness and accreditation programmes for information professionals.

Practical Data Science for Information Professionals

David Stuart

facet
publishing

© David Stuart 2020

Published by Facet Publishing
7 Ridgmount Street, London WC1E 7AE
www.facetpublishing.co.uk

Facet Publishing is wholly owned by CILIP: the Library and Information Association.

British Library Cataloguing in Publication Data
A catalogue record for this book is available from the British Library.

ISBN 978-1-78330-344-1 (paperback)
ISBN 978-1-78330-345-8 (hardback)
ISBN 978-1-78330-346-5 (e-book)

First published 2020

Text printed on FSC accredited material.

Typeset from author's files in 10.5/13 pt Revival 565 and Frutiger by Flagholme Publishing Services.
Printed and made in Great Britain by CPI Group (UK) Ltd, Croydon, CR0 4YY.

For my wife,
who always complains I don't include a dedication.

Contents

Figures

Tables

Boxes

Preface

In essence this book is a natural follow-up to my first book, *Facilitating Access to the Web of Data* (Facet Publishing, 2011). Many of the ideas the book discussed are now widely accepted: library and information professionals have an increasingly important role in data management and access, data and data science are now the subject of massive and widespread interest, and the software and tools available have developed massively.

Since the first book was written libraries have become ever more involved in data management and access, and whereas the idea that there are advantages in library and information professionals having basic programming skills may once have been controversial, it is now an increasingly mainstream idea, which is widely acknowledged if not universally accepted. Programming skills are complementary skills rather than new skills, pushing the upper limits of how information professionals can help on the spectrum of data analysis. The changing attitude is reflected by including a few code examples throughout the book. It is not necessary for the reader to read or follow all these examples, but information professionals should be aware that there is much more that they can do if they are willing to step away from the comfort of the graphical user interface and engage directly with the data, and the easiest way to do this is by acquiring some basic programming skills. As will be seen throughout this book, in the intervening years it has also become much easier to write and share code.

The importance and potential of data is also more widely recognised than when *Facilitating Access to the Web of Data* was first published. Data scientist was not labelled the 'sexiest job of the 21st century' (Davenport and Patil, 2012) until the following year, when 'big data' also burst into public consciousness. Whereas data science was only mentioned once in *Facilitating Access to the Web of Data*, and big data not at all, unsurprisingly the terms are explored far more thoroughly in this book as librarians are increasingly expected to do more than merely facilitate access to the data that is available, but help analyse, visualise and interpret it. The promise and threat of artificial intelligence are more widely recognised than they were in 2011, and the tools are now available to put some of its power in librarians' hands with just a few lines of code.

The resources available have changed considerably since the first book was written: a greater quantity of data and number of tools are now available. The extremely user-friendly Yahoo! Pipes may have plumbed its last data in 2015, but the web is now awash with open source tools and programming libraries that are far more powerful than anything that was available in 2011. Information professionals willing to explore these tools can do much more than facilitate access, but it requires an openness to the new and a willingness to explore and experiment with the tools as they emerge.

Data science is the process by which the power of data is realised, it is how we find actionable insights from among the swathes of data that is available. In an increasingly complex landscape people need help to find these insights (unless we are to sit idly by and watch the digital divide increase) and I believe library and information professionals are ideally positioned to offer that help, to bridge the gap between the human and the data. This book is designed to offer the intrepid information professional the first few practical steps onto the lifelong journey of data science.

What is data science?

'Data! data! data!', he cried impatiently. 'I can't make bricks without clay.'
(Sherlock Holmes in *The Adventure of the Copper Breeches*)

It is well known that we live in an age of unprecedented access to vast quantities of data, and that analysis of this data can produce insights that may be extremely valuable. Less well known is how to analyse the data to gain those insights. That is the topic of data science and this book. This first chapter explores what data science is, some of the drivers behind the rapid increase in data, and how it can be applied within the library and beyond.

By the end of this chapter the reader will be able to see the value of data science beyond the hype, and its widespread applicability within the library and information sector.

Data, information, knowledge, wisdom

Definitions of data science invariably incorporate terms such as data, information or knowledge:

Data analysis and Data Science attempt to extract information from data.
(Idris, 2014, 1)

Data science is a set of fundamental principles that guide the extraction of knowledge from data.
(Provost and Fawcett, 2013, 2)

Data science – the ability to extract knowledge and insights from large and complex data sets.
(Patil, 2015)

So before we attempt to answer the question 'What is data science?', first we must understand what data is, and how it relates to the data–information–

knowledge–wisdom (DIKW) hierarchy that is so often discussed by the library and information science community.

The DIKW model, popularised by Ackoff (1989), creates the hierarchy as a pyramid, with each stage building on the one below, with data at the base. In reality, however, the terms are often used with wide ranging and overlapping definitions (Rowley, 2007; Zins, 2007) and such a bottom-up approach fails to reflect the complexity of how information, knowledge and wisdom are actually derived as it relies too much on the data foundations (Frické, 2009). Of course, 'all models are wrong, but some are useful' (Box and Draper, 1987), and the fact that the DIKW model is wrong does not mean it is totally without value.

Definitions for the terms in the DIKW model may overlap and there is not a simple hierarchy from data through information and knowledge to wisdom, but there is nonetheless a spectrum from data to wisdom and some information and knowledge that can be extracted from data. At the data end of the spectrum we are referring to the facts derived from the world out there, while at the wisdom end of the spectrum we are referring to a person's ability to make good judgements. The process from data to wisdom is not always linear; we do not constantly analyse the world anew based solely on the data in front of us, we see it through the prism of information and knowledge that has already been derived from the world. That does not mean that information, knowledge and wisdom can't be built on data foundations, rather that we need to recognise the role information, knowledge and wisdom have on selecting these foundations and how we interpret the data.

The etymology of 'data' suggests that data are the things that can be measured and recorded from different phenomena, although it is generally used to refer to things that have been captured from all the things it would be possible to capture (Kitchin, 2014). It is an important distinction as there is a huge gap between what could be measured and recorded about a phenomenon and what is measured and recorded. Beyond fundamental limits of what it is possible to know about the physical world, as recognised in Heisenberg's uncertainty principle (the more you know about the exact position of a particle the less you know about its momentum, and vice-versa), there are also a myriad of decisions made about which data is captured, recorded and analysed. These decisions reflect political as well as practical considerations.

For different people working in different fields the data that is captured and is of interest differs considerably. It can differ considerably in size; from the hundreds of petabytes (10^{15}) of data captured by the Large Hadron Collider (Gaillard and Pandolfi, 2017) to the kilobytes (10^3) that may contain the findings of a social science survey. Data may be captured from the real world, derived from an existing data source, or combined from multiple sources. Data may be readily accessible to a person (e.g. in a photograph) or require a large amount of interpretation (e.g. data from the Large Hadron Collider). Data can also mean very different things to different people. For example, the same digitised scientific notebook provides very different data to the historian, the scientist and the social scientist.

Within this book, in true circular style, data is whatever the input for data science is. It is important to recognise the difference between what has been captured and what could be captured, and equally the changing nature of what could be captured through technological progress, but this book is primarily interested in what has been captured, and how that may be used in the discovery of new information, knowledge and eventually wisdom. This book is also primarily interested in the potential of data science that has been enabled by the rapid growth in data in recent years, data that is available in digital form, where new insights may be contained from computational analysis.

Data everywhere

The fast rise in the quantity of data has been variously referred to as a dataquake (Alpaydin, 2016) and a data deluge (Anderson, 2008). How rapid the rise has been, or how much data now exists, is difficult to quantify because of the myriad of different ways such a question may be answered. How much data is stored is different from how much data is consumed, which is different again from technology's capacity to store or carry data (Hilbert, 2015). What is clear, however, whatever the measure used, is that there has been a data revolution (Kitchin, 2014) and we live in the age of big data (Manyika et al., 2011) where data is ever more notable for three properties: volume, velocity and variety (Sagiroglu and Sinanc, 2013).

The rapid increase in data is a natural consequence of the digital transformation of much of our working and personal lives. Most visibly in the headline catching numbers of people creating and sharing content on social media sites (e.g. Facebook, YouTube) or smart phone apps (e.g. WhatsApp, Instagram), but also in the quick rise in the technical specifications of tools and instruments, and the less visible trails hidden from view.

A more thorough overview of some of the data that is available is provided in Chapter 2, but for now let us consider the example of the data that may be generated by a simple trip to a shop for a pint of milk. Not that long ago such an event would have been unremarkable, notable only by the amount of milk left in the shop and cash in the till at the end of the day. Now the fact that we are leaving home may be registered by our increasingly smart homes, as smart devices are turned off, our virtual assistants note a lack of noise in the house, and our smart meter registers a fall in electricity consumption. Our smart watches and phones register the fact that we are moving, count our steps, and share our changing location with the telephone company and those smart phone apps that have requested the necessary permission on installation (irrespective of whether it is core to their functionality). If we drive to the shop our increasingly smart cars may log our journey, oil level, petrol consumption and a host of other pieces of data that are uploaded to the car manufacturer or our insurance company. The journey may also be tracked by cameras and sensors as our ever smarter cities monitor traffic flows and pollution levels. Finally, at the shop the transaction is more and more likely to take place electronically; this may provide the shop with another data point for the shop's profile of the customer, the transaction is shared with the customer's bank and payment company, the shop's stock is automatically updated and the data possibly cascaded down the supply chain.

Examples of such chains and webs of data are ubiquitous in today's world, and with so much data available businesses and organisations of all types are trying to extract value, or enable others to extract value, from it. Governments are opening up some of their vast data sets to the public, not only in response to calls for greater transparency but as a way to release the value of the data. Researchers are opening up their data to reduce duplication, improve its quality, and maximise the value of publicly funded research. Businesses are increasingly storing vast quantities of disparate data in data warehouses in the hope that it can one day be mined for useful nuggets of information.

Although there are vast quantities of data being captured, and a portion of this data is being shared, that alone is not enough for its value to be realised. Without the necessary tools and methodologies to turn this data into actionable knowledge possible opportunities and insights are being wasted. As John Naisbitt (1984, 17) put it before the current deluge: 'We are drowning in information, but starved for knowledge.' Data science refers to the tools and methodologies that try to use the data and turn it into actionable knowledge. It is important to recognise, however, that there continues to be great swathes of data that is either not captured or not shared.

The data deserts

This book is about the rapid rise in the amount of data that is available and the tools that can use it, but we should nonetheless pause to reflect on the data deserts. There continue to be great swathes of data that is either not captured or not shared. This is not only for technical and business reasons, but also for political and economic reasons. History is replete with examples of the misuse of data that has been collected, but it is also important to be aware of what is not being collected and its implications.

Governments collect vast amounts of data, but the data they collect may make them look bad, require action they are not willing to take, or require investment they are not willing to make. Ahead of the 2016 Rio Olympics a project by Google and the non-profit AfroReggae mapped some of the favelas surrounding Rio (Matcher, 2016); such mapping and the wider collection of data on favelas is an important part of ensuring that people can be seen to have access to the public services that they require.

There are also many communities whose members are unable to benefit from the data deluge, to take advantage of insights available through data science because there is less adoption of smart technology, a lack of infrastructure to share the data, and few resources to analyse it. Data science is part of a wider information ecosystem, subject to government policies, social practices and individual whims echoing through the system. Gurstein (2011) identifies seven elements necessary for people to use open data effectively: internet; computers and software; computer and software skills; content and formatting; interpretation and sense making; advocacy; and governance. If any of those elements is lacking, an organisation, a research discipline, a community, or even a whole country will quickly be left behind.

The library community has always had an important role in widening access to resources, and this includes increased access to data. It may be perfectly acceptable that we don't have detailed weather forecasts for planets in far off galaxies or that Amazon doesn't want to share all its transactional data; less acceptable may be the consequences for those who are left behind from the data advantage. The library community cannot necessarily level the playing field, but it can take steps to alleviate some of the worst inequalities: helping users manage the data that is available, and drawing attention to those areas where marginalised groups are particularly affected by a lack of freely available data.

Data science

This book is not about the data that is missing, but rather the data that is available and how data science can be used to discover new information and knowledge. Data science has become a bit of a buzz phrase, helped no doubt by 'data scientist' being described as the 'sexiest job of the 21st century' in the *Harvard Business Review* (Davenport and Patil, 2012). In this book Provost and Fawcett's (2013, 2) definition of data science is taken: 'a set of fundamental principles that guide the extraction of knowledge from data'. It is not limited to the traditional realm of science, but rather reflects the need for data scientists to design equipment, gather data, conduct experiments and communicate results (Davenport and Patil, 2012).

There has been a steady growth in interest in data science in recent years, as can be seen in the number of Google searches on the topic (Figure 1.1).

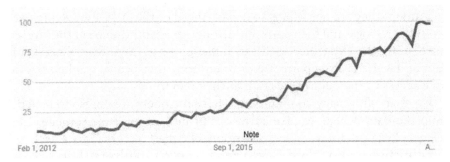

Figure 1.1 *Google Trends chart showing the steady growth in the use of the term 'data science' in Google Search between February 2012 and April 2019;* Google and the Google logo are registered trademarks of Google Inc., used with permission

The y-axis represents search interest relative to the highest point on the graph, so we can see there have been approximately ten times as many 'data science' searches in 2019 as 2012. This may reflect the growing number of case studies and examples where the use of data science has led to significant improvements in required outcomes, but also the increased access to data and data tools. For example, Figure 1.1 not only shows the growth in interest in data science, but also demonstrates the vast quantities of data that can be simply queried over the internet, as anyone with internet access can now explore billions of search queries. Google Trends in particular provides access to the sort of insights into the human psyche that would have been impossible before we moved so much of our lives online (Stephens-Davidowitz, 2018).

Many of the most notable data science examples come from the technology sector (e.g. Netflix, Amazon and Google), where vast quantities of data collide with large numbers of workers with the requisite statistical and computational expertise.

Google's early adoption of the PageRank algorithm (Brin and Page, 1998), where network analysis of the graph of linked web pages was used to identify the most relevant web pages, quickly led them to search engine market dominance. Amazon's market dominance is often attributed to its recommendations algorithm, which is based on what the current customer and other users have viewed and purchased (Mangalindan, 2012). Between 2006 and 2009 Netflix ran the Netflix Prize challenge (www.netflixprize.com) to find out how to improve predictions about how much someone would enjoy a film, demonstrating the power of data science to improve services, and the potential of crowdsourcing solutions by making data publicly available. Higher education is not only being changed by the impact of massive open online courses (MOOCs), but the move to provide content online in increasingly bite-sized chunks enables content and courses to be analysed at levels of granulation that it had never been analysed at before (Waldrop, 2013).

There are many noteworthy examples of data science being employed away from the big technology companies. Duhigg (2012) highlights how the US retailer Target has used sales data to identify pregnant customers who are considered to be particularly valuable (albeit not always to the appreciation of customers). Higher education institutions are increasingly using learning analytics to boost student retention (Sclater and Mullan, 2017) and cities are using data science to improve response times by the police and other emergency services.

Such a broad range of applications leaves 'data science' at risk of becoming a meaningless phrase, after all, aren't all researchers supposed to extract knowledge from data? This has led many data science discussions to focus on the key skills of data scientists, and how they differ from more established roles. Often these have taken the form of Venn diagrams (or at least Venn-type diagrams) (Taylor, 2016), variously emphasising data scientists' principal areas of expertise. Davenport and Patil (2012) describe the data scientist as 'a hybrid of data hacker, analyst, communicator, and trust advisor'.

Here we consider three of those areas of expertise:

- domain expertise
- mathematical and statistical knowledge
- coding and hacking skills.

Domain expertise does not distinguish data scientists from traditional researchers, and nor does the application of mathematical and statistical techniques, however the complexity of the mathematical and statistical techniques applied, and their combination with coding and hacking skills, undoubtedly do. The application of these mathematical and coding techniques cut across domains so data scientists within different domains may have more in common with one another than with those working in the same domain. For example, a data scientist in a social science department may have more in common with a business analyst in the private sector than more qualitative social scientists within their own department.

Within data science there is a greater emphasis on the extraction of knowledge from data than in other disciplines. As was mentioned above, one of the criticisms of the DIKW model is that much knowledge and wisdom does not follow a linear route through from data. Within data science there is a greater emphasis on such a route than traditional approaches to research.

Several related terms may be applied to the extraction of knowledge from data, referring to the application of specific technologies or methodologies, use in a particular domain, or simply a rebranding in the hype cycle. A practical introduction to data science should not get too bogged down with the subtleties between the different terms, or indeed the subtleties between different people's definitions of the different terms, but a brief introduction to the terms can help to flesh out the realms of data science:

- *Business analytics*: As the term suggests, business analytics is the application of statistical techniques for analysing and improving business services.
- *Data-driven science*: Whereas data science can refer to the application of the data science methodology to any sector, data-driven science is generally applied more specifically to the discovery of knowledge from data in the scientific domain.
- *Data mining*: Data mining is about the storage of vast quantities of data, and then searching for nuggets. Data science is typically more human-centric than data mining, with data scientists going out and finding what they are looking for.
- *Machine learning*: Machine learning is an approach to knowledge discovery, and may be applied in data science, data-driven science, business analytics or data mining.

Some of these terms (e.g. machine learning) are explored in detail later in the book.

By its nature language is fluid, and the definitions above will fail to satisfy everyone and inevitably shift over time. Nonetheless, they begin to show the scope and potential of data science.

The potential of data science

The potential of data science varies considerably according to how and where the data science tools and methodologies are applied. Data science may be a relatively small internal affair, where an organisation's internal databases are used to inform customer segmentation and improve sales. Alternatively data scientists may use public data from across the web to gain insights into attitudes and trends around the world. There again it may be used to analyse the DNA of millions of patients to gain insights into the genetic disposition to certain diseases. The potential for data science is huge; the frontiers are moving rapidly as new data and algorithms emerge, and the value of data science has only begun to be realised. We must be wary, though, of falling for Silicon Valley's tendency to techno-utopianism. However much data is captured, it will not reflect the true complexity of the real world, and it is not, as Anderson (2008) suggested, the end of theory.

The potential and limits of data science can most clearly be seen in an area such as online searching, which exemplifies the scale of computational analysis that is necessary and possible. Search companies and social network sites, some of which may be considered search engines (Bradley, 2017), have developed extensive big data frameworks and infrastructures to deal with the rapid growth in the data they need to analyse. The success of online searching is demonstrated through the growth of searching in our everyday lives, providing ever more relevant and personalised results as and when we need them. But search engines also demonstrate the limits of data science, caused by the underlying data and the interests of the companies analysing it.

Searching is now ubiquitous online, and it is difficult to imagine a time when human-indexed directories were a rival for finding information on the web; the thoughtful assessment and curation of online content by humans has all but been superseded in every area by the brute force of indexing of search engines. A few carefully chosen keywords can now produce 'good enough' personalised results in less than a second, which get users returning to a website again and again. That Google is now estimated to answer over a trillion queries a year (Bradley, 2017) is testament to the power of the search engines. The results are not perfect, but recall has taken precedence over precision, and with content being continually created throughout the world a human-centred alternative is inconceivable.

As well as indexing ever larger quantities of information increasingly quickly (as users expect the latest news and social network content to be immediately indexed by search engines), search engines have also produced ancillary services providing access and insights into specific types of resources. Google Trends (https://trends.google.com) provides access to information about search behaviour over time, which can be used to predict everything from the winners of celebrity talent shows (Tancer, 2009) to the spread of diseases (Eysenbach, 2006). For example, searches for pornography potentially offer an early indicator of unemployment rates, as there is a correlation between the two, and the number of people searching for pornography is available before the official unemployment figures are collated (Stephens-Davidowitz, 2018). Google Books Ngram Viewer (https://books.google.com/ngrams) provides frequencies of terms in printed resources between 1500 and 2008, and Silver (2012) has shown how the terms 'predictable' and 'unpredictable' were influenced in the 20th century by the Second World War. Microsoft Academic Search (https://academic.microsoft.com) is a bibliographic database with application programming interface (API) access enabling researchers to send queries for bibliometric research freely and automatically.

Although search engines collect an increasing amount of data, it can only ever be a partial representation of reality. Keywords lack the context of language used in a conversation between people in the real world. Language is ambiguous, especially when reduced to two or three keywords; is 'Apple' the fruit, the record label, or the technology company? Users are also ambiguous; as well as the problem of distinguishing between different people, the same person behaves differently in different situations. Search engines try to include context with log-ins, personalisation, and the capturing of geolocation information, but a single user may have multiple profiles or the same log-in profiles may be used by multiple users. Although Mark Zuckerberg famously claimed that 'having two identities for yourself is an example of a lack of integrity' (Bort, 2014), most accept that it is perfectly normal for people to want to separate out different parts of their lives. This is increasingly reflected in more restrictive data laws, e.g. the General Data Protection Regulations (GDPR), and a pivot by social media companies, with even Mark Zuckerberg now stating, 'The future is private' (Wong, 2019). Unfortunately for search engines this contributes to the fact that there is always a gap between what users think and how they express their thoughts in keywords.

Finally, it is important to remember that the interests of search companies are not the same as the interests of users. The job of most search engines is not to help you find what you are looking for, but to keep you coming back often enough to sell the advertising (Bradley, 2017). The perfect search engine, for which the top result provides the perfect answer, would inevitably sell less advertising than the search engine which has the perfect answer below the advertising. Equally, it is in YouTube's interests that a user watches multiple videos rather than the single video that they may have initially been looking for.

The search industry has successfully analysed vast quantities of data to improve its primary service (which depending on your perspective is either providing access to information or selling advertising) while also discovering new knowledge, from predicting American Idol winners to flu outbreaks. Similar opportunities for improvements and the discovery of new knowledge are available in every industry, including the information profession, and luckily there are opportunities to gain these insights without always requiring the building of extensive big data frameworks and infrastructures.

From research data services to data science in libraries

Libraries, especially academic and research libraries, have increasingly offered data services in recent years, but it is important to distinguish between the provision of data services and the provision of data science. A library may provide the infrastructure for supporting researchers with the long-term preservation of data, but data analysis requires very different technical skills from data preservation (Xia and Wang, 2014), and the provision of one does not necessarily indicate an ability or wish to provide the other.

The data services offered by a library may be categorised in different ways. Reznik-Zellen, Adamick and McGinty (2012) identified three tiers of research data support services: education, where libraries educate their users about data management; consultation, where libraries consult with researchers and data management issues; and infrastructure, where libraries provide the infrastructure for data management and curation. Similarly, Si et al. (2015) identified six types of service the world's top university libraries typically offer: introducing research data, giving guidelines on data management planning, data curation and storage service, data management training, data management reference training and recommending resources.

Si et al. (2015) investigated 87 of the world's top 100 universities, and identified 50 (57%) that offered research data services. Information and consultative services are found more often than technical services (Tenopir et al., 2015, 2017), and a survey of the directors of the Association of European Research Libraries found that less than half (40.9%) said they had policies in their libraries relating to research data services. Nonetheless, irrespective of whether or not their libraries offered research data services, directors overwhelmingly agreed that libraries need to offer them to remain relevant (Tenopir et al., 2017).

The provision of these services may be considered to fall under the role of 'data librarianship', one of four data-related roles identified by Swan and Brown (2008), the others being data creator, data scientist and data manager. Whereas data librarians specialise in the curation and preservation of data, data scientists work with the data, although as the concept of the data life cycle becomes more important it is increasingly recognised that data preservation cannot simply be wrapped up at the end of a research project (Xia and Wang, 2014). Data scientists' skills have been suggested as the foundation for data librarians. Semeler, Pinto and Rozandos (2017, 772) proposed that 'librarians should refer to data science when seeking to develop practical and theoretical skills for data management and data curation', while Xia and Wang (2014) have said that data librarians share the same skills as well as facilitation and communication skills.

There is, undoubtedly, some overlap between data librarians and data scientists, with some shared skills and knowledge. An understanding of curation and preservation practices undoubtedly helps data scientists find and use the data they require, while data science methodologies potentially provide library and information professionals, including data librarians, with new insights into their work and the work of data scientists. Cox (2018) has suggested there is a spectrum of data roles, from those roles familiar in librarians (e.g. supporting data search and access) to those that are unfamiliar (e.g. data analysis and visualisation). Similarly Burton et al. (2018) have suggested that data science exists on a spectrum, from advocacy and evidence-based decision making to advanced statistical and software engineering.

Data science is a growth area ideal for library and information professionals to pursue. The focus is often on the 'mathematical and statistical' and 'coding and hacking' parts of the skill set, but equally important are the domain knowledge and the strong 'social skills' (Davenport and Patil, 2012) that have long been part of the librarian's skill set, and the need to combine all available online and offline resources (Stephens-Davidowitz, 2018). They are 'ideally situated to serve academia, government, and business as information collectors, curators, and analysts' (NMC, 2017, 38). Like librarianship, data science can suffer from an image problem, with data scientists being reduced to mere number crunchers, but like librarians a data scientist is 'a high-ranking professional with the training and curiosity to make discoveries in the world of big data' (Davenport and Patil, 2012).

Not everyone has been enthusiastic about information professionals having a data-centric vision. As Frické (2009, 135) notes, 'The information scientist does not want to be collecting data hoping that it might be promoted to information.' There is much to be said for a top down just in time approach to certain data collection, but there are also vast quantities of data that is available or easily accessible and potentially highly valuable, and librarians have an important role in facilitating access and analysis of it (NITRD, 2016). Some have suggested there is a role for library and information professionals in the area of text and data mining, building on their understanding of intellectual property law (Secker et al., 2016). As Burton and Lyon (2017) point out, however, there is a technical skills gap, and it may be difficult for libraries to find librarians with the full range of data services skills (Tenopir et al., 2015). There are a number of initiatives trying to help close this gap: Data Science Training for Librarians (www.dst4l.info), the Data Science and Visualization Institute for Librarians (www.lib.ncsu.edu/data-science-and-visualization-institute) and Library Carpentry (https://librarycarpentry.github.io).

As may be deduced from the title of this book, *Practical Data Science for Information Professionals*, the author falls firmly on the side of opinion that sees library and information professionals having an important role to play in the future of data science, ensuring that users have access to the data as and when they need it in the form that they need it. It is not something altogether new to librarianship, but may already be touched on in areas such as competitive intelligence or bibliometrics. As has been argued elsewhere, Ranganathan's five laws of library science may be applied equally to the data age:

1 Data is for use.
2 Every user their data.
3 Every data its user.
4 Save the time of the user.
5 The web of data is a growing organism.

(Stuart, 2011, 139)

The data ecosystem is complex, and those who need access to data, or would benefit from the insights that may be derived from the data, do not always have the requisite skills. Information professionals have an opportunity to provide the necessary support, helping users to analyse data that is available, and working alongside researchers assisting them with their data management throughout the research process, librarian as 'co-investigator, not an overhead' (Ekstrøm et al., 2016). Libraries offer different levels of service: a well-financed university library has more scope than a single special librarian in a commercial company. But there is also a place for data scientists to apply data science tools and methodologies for their own professional ends, and even if librarians never have the opportunity to provide data services to the wider organisation, there are advantages in them having at least a cursory understanding of the field.

Bibliometrics, 'the application of mathematics and statistical methods to books and other media of communication' (Pritchard, 1969, 349), is a well-established area of library and information science, and these types of studies may now be enhanced with the new sources of data available online. The clustering of researchers to provide insights into research interests rather than institutional structure could be provided through a network analysis of the publication data in a library's research information system, data about books borrowed in a library's integrated library system, or the friending on a public social network site. Trend analysis may consider seasonal variation to provide insights into the future popularity of certain topics, the basis of a foresight study, or even the future of the library itself.

Bibliomining has been suggested as a term for evidence-based librarianship using large sets of library data (Nicholson, 2006a, 2006b). Bibliomining combines bibliometrics and data mining, gathering the disparate sources of data into a data warehouse for analysis as and when necessary. Library data may be combined with other university data to determine whether library use correlates with academic grades, and where appropriate help to demonstrate the impact of library services where library use correlates with higher grades (Renaud et al., 2015). Book borrowing statistics can help to determine the useful life of a book and when they may be moved to remote storage (Renaud et al., 2015). Groups of libraries can share their data so the impact of different policies in different libraries can be compared (Nicholson, 2006a).

Programming in libraries

The importance of information professionals being able to program is as contentious as the idea of information professionals as data scientists. Content analyses of job adverts have found that programming skills are rarely a requirement (Mathews and Pardue, 2009; Raju, 2017), despite 70–75% of library jobs requiring advanced IT skills (Raju, 2017). However, growing recognition of the importance of programming can be seen in the interest in makerspaces and code clubs in libraries (Kroski, 2017), so it is not unreasonable to expect to see an increasing need for information professionals to know how to program in the future.

It is not necessary for information scientists to be able to program; there is a variety of proprietary and open source software available for data science analysis that requires no programming. This includes tools for scraping the web, cleaning the data and analysing it (see Chapter 4, 'Tools for data analysis'). One of the most popular data science tools is Excel, used by 28.1% of those respondents to the annual KDnuggets survey aimed at the data mining and science community (Piatetsky, 2017). However, when using existing software you are generally limited to the functionality imagined by the software creators, and may be limited by an interface that doesn't scale well to a large data set or where data requires multiple manipulations. Also, knowing the basics of programming may help in your understanding of the limitations of any software you use or the algorithms that increasingly dictate which information we see online. Even limited coding skills can go a long way.

Studying how to program can seem a steep learning curve to the uninitiated, a complex world with a host of unintelligible languages and excessive quantities of punctuation. Even choosing which language to use can seem an overwhelming task as there are hundreds of languages available. However, you no more need to have advanced programming skills to start manipulating data than you need to understand macros and Visual Basic for Applications (VBA) to use Excel, or need to be a fluent French speaker to ask your way to a train station in Paris. Rather than data carpentry we should be considering data bricolage; information professionals don't need to be professional programmers, but like bricoleurs can use 'devious means compared to those of the craftsman' (Lévis-Strauss, 1966, 16–17). The web is full of example code from which to cobble together solutions to most coding problems.

As this book will show, even a limited amount of programming opens up a host of possibilities in data science.

Programming in this book

This book is not, and in no way should be mistaken for, an introduction to programming, but it includes coding examples to ease the practical application of some of the ideas expressed in this book. The coding examples come in one of two languages: Python or R. There are hundreds of programming languages available, but in most cases the choice is really just one of a handful, and Python and R are the two most popular software tools among data scientists (Piatetsky, 2017). Most programming languages can be dismissed as simply as someone considering a second language would dismiss the options of Esperanto and Klingon, although if the reader wishes to explore the variety of languages available, look at 99 Bottles of Beer (www.99-bottles-of-beer.net), which provides code examples for over 1,500 languages (all of which print the lyrics to 99 bottles of beer).

Python is one of the most popular programming languages within the data science community (Piatetsky, 2017) and more widely (Cass, 2017). It is a high level programming language, easy to understand by people as well as computers, and is often the first language introduced in schools after the drag-and-drop block-based languages such as Scratch (https://scratch.mit.edu) or Blockly (https://developers.google.com/blockly). As there is a large user base there are many books and resources on learning the software, various integrated development environments in which to program, and libraries of code which have been published for reuse.

R is not as popular (Cass, 2017) nor as intuitive as Python, but is widely used within the data science community thanks to the comprehensiveness of the statistical packages, which provide quick and powerful analysis of large data sets.

A very short introduction to the software for both languages can be found in the back of this book (see Appendix), along with recommendations for further reading. Programming is also returned to in Chapter 4, 'Tools for data analysis', where the languages are considered in some detail, along with some of the principal libraries likely to be of interest to information professionals as data scientists. Although the book includes programming examples, it is not necessary to follow the examples when reading it, or indeed to return to them at any point, to understand the fundamentals of data science.

The structure of this book

The rest of the book is broadly split into three parts: chapters 2–4 provide an overview of data science data, methods and tools; chapters 5–7 consider specific methodologies in more detail; and Chapter 8 considers the future of data science and information professionals.

Chapter 2, 'Little data, big data', provides an overview of the range of data that is increasingly available and how it may be used in an information professional's work.

Chapter 3, 'The process of data science', discusses the data science method: data collection, data cleaning, analysis and visualisation. It provides examples of how the stages can be applied practically in the information profession.

Chapter 4, 'Tools for data analysis', considers some data analysis tools, including the programming languages and packages that make previously complex analysis increasingly accessible.

Chapter 5, 'Clustering and social network analysis', discusses some of the main clustering and social network analysis methodologies, their potential application by information professionals, and how they can be calculated to provide evaluative and relational insights.

Chapter 6, 'Predictions and forecasts', looks at some of the main methodologies for making predictions, and how such forecasting methodologies may be applied by information professionals.

Chapter 7, 'Text analysis and mining', considers how the increasingly large quantities of unstructured text data can form the basis of text analysis and mining techniques, and how information professionals can use them.

Chapter 8, 'The future of data science and information professionals', considers the future growth of data science and the role of information professionals as they continue to reposition themselves in the changing information ecosystem.

2

Little data, big data

Today there are vast quantities and varieties of data, with new data sources emerging all the time. This makes any attempt to provide an overview of data a futile and quickly outdated task. Therefore this chapter considers some of the data that is available according to three features: whether it is 'big data', its format, and its source.

'Big data' is typically used to describe the large quantities of data now being generated and the complex infrastructure needed for their collection and analysis, and it can be contrasted with small data sets that can be simply gathered and analysed on a desktop. Data format provides an overview of some of the ways data can appear, from tables of data in documents through to APIs and linked data. Finally data sources looks more closely at some of the sources of data that are currently publicly available, as well as some of the additional data a library or information professional may have access to.

Big data

The term 'big data' can be traced back to the mid-1990s (Kitchin and McArdle, 2016), although it really entered the public consciousness in 2012. *The New York Times* ran articles with titles such as 'The Age of Big Data' (Lohr, 2012a) and 'How Big Data Became So Big' (Lohr, 2012b); the *Guardian* had 'Why Big Data is Now Such a Big Deal' (Naughton, 2012b) and 'Big Data: revolution by numbers' (Naughton, 2012a); and *Big Data, Big Impact* (WEF, 2012) was a topic at Davos in 2012. Google Trends shows there was a rapid rise in online searches for the term over the year, and since then there has been a raft of popular science and business publications devoted to the subject: *Big Data* (Mayer-Schönberger and Cukier, 2013); *Big Data* (Marr, 2015); *Big Data for Small Business for Dummies* (Marr, 2016); and *Big Data: does size matter?* (Harkness, 2016).

Despite the rapid growth in the popularity of big data, pinning down what is meant by the term is more difficult. Although it was initially used to refer to situations where the volume of data had grown so large that it no longer fitted into a computer's processing memory (Mayer-Schönberger and Cukier,

2013), as computers have become more powerful (Moore's law) and for a long time memory got much cheaper (Kryder's law) (Rosenthal, 2017), such usage is crude as these situations are moveable targets: what is considered big data one day may not be big data the next.

Rather than considering the absolute size of big data, the challenge is to analyse it for meaningful insights. Laney (2001) identified three growing data management challenges, and these have since been widely seen as traits of big data: its volume, velocity and variety. There are now enormous volumes of data available for analysis about ever more specific areas of our lives. This data is increasingly up to date. Whereas a census may have taken place every ten years, and market research data have taken weeks to gather and analyse, now research can be carried out and data gathered in near real time. The internet brings together a wide range of data in the same place, from vast quantities of unstructured documents to highly structured data adhering to agreed international standards.

The three Vs of big data have since been extended to include various other traits, including exhaustivity, resolution and indexicality, relationality, and extensionality and scalability (Kitchin and McArdle, 2016), although in practice big data sets rarely have all, or even most, of the traits. Kitchin and McArdle's (2016) analysis of 26 data sets, each of which was considered to be big data, found that many possessed neither volume nor variety, and that velocity and exhaustivity were the principal markers of big data: the internet allows data to be collected and shared in near real time, and as everyone's data is shared we move from small sample sizes to n=all.

A more useful description of big data is 'things one can do at a large scale that cannot be done at a smaller one, to extract new insights or create new forms of value' (Mayer-Schönberger and Cukier, 2013, 6). This not only includes big, real-time and exhaustive data sets, but may include the combining of multiple small data sets. For example, over 100 scientists sharing GPS data on the migration patterns of animals enables insights that would be impossible by any single researcher (Marris, 2018). Big data enables the zooming in on small sub-sets of the data (Stephens-Davidowitz, 2018). For example, national opinion polling for a general election with a sample size of 1000–2000 only has a margin of error of 2–3%, but it would not allow you to zoom in and draw conclusions about any particular constituency.

From a data science perspective, the size of the data is not particularly important, and we should be wary of focusing on big data at the expense of small data: 'The solution is not always more Big Data. A special sauce is often necessary to help Big Data work best: the judgement of humans and small surveys, what we might call small data' (Stephens-Davidowitz, 2018, 254–5).

Although there are practical implications for the computer power necessary as we move from analysing megabytes through gigabytes to terabytes and petabytes, more important is the accompanying change in mindset from one of data scarcity to one of data abundance.

From the perspective of the data's ability to fit in the memory of a computer for processing, the focus of this work is primarily on small data. This is likely to be most information professionals' experience of data science. Where there is big data it is generally hidden from view, accessible via a web service, and the scientific analysis is performed on small data sets. If we want to understand the feelings of the general population on various topics, we do not need to build a robust infrastructure that regularly interrupts people to ask them their opinion, we are more likely to tap into the data from a social network site, query its API, and analyse the portion of data that we need on our regular desktop. It is important to recognise the impact of the GDPR legislation on access to big data, especially social media data, and we may increasingly be moving to a post-big data world.

Data formats

Data is everywhere and organisations have several information systems and software that can talk to each other to different extents. Some software has export functionality, some has APIs, and some has functionality for building and searching according to common languages, e.g. Structured Query Language (SQL) or Simple Protocol and RDF Query Language (SPARQL).

The focus here is not on the infrastructure that ensures that the data is accessible, but the different ways it is made accessible. The challenge of distributing the petabytes that emerge from the Large Hadron Collider in the seconds after impact, or the thousands of updates published on Twitter every minute, are obviously very different from the sharing of survey results from a social survey. For the most part, this is immaterial to information professionals. In the same way as you do not need to be aware of how the water gets to your tap, just how you can turn it on, you don't need to know the machinations of a Twitter server farm, just how you can download the data that you need.

As every office has a different set of software, here the discussion focuses primarily on some of the data that is available on the world wide web. The types of data are by no means restricted to the world wide web, plenty of widely used software allows for exporting the data into popular and non-proprietary formats, or provides an API to enable integration with other software. It is simply that a description of the data analysis functionality of a myriad of different types of software would be too specific to be widely applicable, and extremely turgid.

Standalone files

Big data may have captured all the headlines, but we should not overlook standalone data files, which may be exported from the services we use, sitting on our desktops, or have been shared on the web. COUNTER statistics may be downloaded from a publisher's website for insights into the return on investment from library subscriptions; a library's Twitter archive may be downloaded to discover the characteristics of the most successful tweets; publicly shared data from similar institutions may provide new insights or comparisons for a library. Standalone files can come from an endless variety of sources in an endless variety of formats, but most importantly the data is not tied to the system where it was captured or created, but can be exported and shared in a small, manageable number of files.

These files may be in a proprietary format, with the data only accessible by the same software that created it, but ideally it is in an open format enabling the data to be combined, manipulated and analysed in new ways.

Often these standalone files are tables of data such as Excel spreadsheets, comma-separated values (CSVs) or tab-delineated files, although data may just as easily be marked-up as Extensible Mark-up Language (XML) or JavaScript Object Notation (JSON). The table of data, however, is most people's experience of structured data, and while tables may easily be overlooked among the glitz and glamour of mammoth data sets and interconnectivity, they nevertheless have the advantage that they provide a simple way to access and share data that can be easily comprehended. In comparison, other formats that may require knowledge of additional software or the structure of the data to start using it, a table of data may be simply opened with familiar spreadsheet software, or in the case of CSVs and tab-delineated files a simple text editor such as Windows Notepad.

Spreadsheets are the low lying fruit of data sharing. If a spreadsheet is created using online software, such as Google Sheets, publication is as simple as changing the access settings, so that it is public on the web and anyone can find and view it. Alternatively, there is now a rich ecosystem of repositories available where people can share their data, from institutional and subject repositories that may place restrictions on the type of data that can be uploaded and who can upload it, to general repositories that allow any data in any format.

This ease of publication comes with disadvantages. There may be limitations on the size and structure of the data that can be shared. Unfortunately, because of the low barrier to publication the accompanying documentation often leaves much to be desired, though this opens up the possibility of creating extremely unusual and idiosyncratic data sets. Responses to a recent request from the Open Data Institute for examples of quirky data sets included the names of all registered dogs in Zurich, a list of which animals break wind, and Peterborough City Council's list of frozen animals (Vryzakis, Scott and Foulds, 2018). Few would consider these data sources worthy of a more sophisticated data infrastructure.

Application programming interfaces

APIs enable users to interact with a service programmatically. For example, if you don't like the web interface of Twitter, or wanted a sensor to send automatic updates to your Twitter account, you can use Twitter's set of APIs to write a program to download or send the updates in the way you wish. The focus in this book is on APIs for accessing data on the web, rather than for updating data or interacting with desktop software. These APIs can give access to more data than could be comfortably downloaded, facilitate analysis of the data, and at the same time leave control of the data with the data publisher.

As has already been mentioned, we live in an age distinguished by being able to access the vast quantities of data available, with many of the data sets beyond the processing power of a desktop computer. This is true not only for high-profile data-intensive fields such as particle physics, but also in fields closer to the interests of library and information professionals, such as webometrics, 'the study of the quantitative aspects of the construction and use of information resources, structures and technologies on the web drawing on bibliometric and informetric approaches' (Björneborn and Ingwersen, 2004, 1217). Data about the web as a whole, as opposed to the small part researchers may be able to crawl for themselves, is essential for many studies. As may be expected, downloading and analysing a copy of the web is extremely resource intensive. In May 2019 a copy of the Common Crawl, a repository of web crawl data, consisted of over 220 tebibytes of data (http://commoncrawl.org/2019/05/may-2019-crawl-archive-now-available), far beyond what could be handled by a desktop computer. A search engine API can provide access to similarly sized data sets, with complex indexing and infrastructure enabling far quicker responses to queries than could be achieved by someone on their own. This comes at a price for data users, however, as they are restricted by the complexity of sending queries and the limitations placed by the external service.

As the 'programming' part of API would suggest, APIs often require a few more specialist skills than are required for downloading a standalone file from the internet. Most of the sort of public data APIs discussed in this book have been made available via representational state transfer (REST) in a RESTful architecture, using the protocols of the web such as HyperText Transfer Protocol (HTTP) for sending requests. Although there are non-RESTful

APIs, e.g. Simple Object Access Protocol and Z39.50, the potential simplicity of RESTful APIs makes them dominant on the web. These APIs are, nonetheless, typically more complicated to use than downloading a file from a website, especially where authentication is a requirement, parameters do not fit neatly into a uniform resource identifier (URI), documentation is limited, or the user wants to combine data from more than one source. Fortunately the software process is being made simpler by the increasing number of software libraries that support the process of downloading data from a particular source. Box 2.1 shows an example of a RESTful API request.

Box 2.1 Example of a RESTful API request

At its most simple an API request is as simple as a URI you might type into a browser address bar. For example, Open Library (http://openlibrary.org), a website with the stated aim of creating one web page for every book ever published, provides a simple RESTful search API (https://openlibrary.org/dev/docs/api/search) which requires no authentication and all the information is contained in the parameters of the URI and can be encoded in an HTTP GET request. The following URI entered into a browser address bar returns metadata in a JSON format of those books that have 'facet' in the publisher field and 'stuart' in the author field:

http://openlibrary.org/search.json?publisher=facet&author=stuart

APIs invariably impose limitations on how the data can be accessed and queried, and the number of queries that can be sent. It should be remembered that the interests of the publisher of the data service are not necessarily the same as those of users of the data service, and functionality may come and go as it suits the publisher or the changing political environment. For example, following the Cambridge Analytica data misuse scandal in 2018, where personal data was harvested for political advertising, Facebook added some restrictions to the APIs (Perez, 2018). While this may be seen as positive for the privacy of user data, it has implications for researchers who wish to investigate an increasingly important part of our cultural environment: researchers in private companies can work in a way that is not possible by those in public institutions.

Unlike the standalone file which can be simply uploaded and shared, in most cases it is more difficult to set up a web API from the perspective of sharing data, though this is not always the case, as online software often comes with existing APIs that may be used. For example, data shared via Google Sheets is accessible via an API as Google Sheets has an extensive range of APIs for accessing data (https://developers.google.com/sheets/api).

Linked data and the semantic web

The big problem with APIs is that they can be very different from one another, and they require an understanding of the idiosyncrasies introduced by the particular individuals who have set them up, whether the structure of the data, the query method or the protocols used to retrieve the data. This has obvious implications when you are trying to scale up and combine data from multiple different websites. The semantic web is a set of protocols for publishing data on the web so that the meaning of the data is explicit, reusing vocabularies and ontologies to give meaning to the concepts and entities that form the basis of the Resource Description Framework (RDF) triple, the basic unit of the semantic web.

The semantic web has seemingly been 'just around the corner' for much of the last 20 years, and while some have become disillusioned with it ever arriving, and a lot of interest has moved to the potential of artificial intelligence (AI), it is important to recognise that semantic web technologies and AI are complementary rather than competing technologies. To over simplify: AI provides the tools to discover new information and knowledge, the semantic web provides a way to represent it. A lot of significant RDF data sets are already available. Linked Open Data (http://lod-cloud.net), which maps large interlinked data sets that follow linked data principles (see below), has grown from 12 in 2007 to 1,239 data sets in 2019. This map does not include the many unlinked and smaller data sets that have been published across the web. This section provides just a simple overview of the semantic web and linked data. A more detailed discussion of these particular technologies for information professionals can be found in *Practical Ontologies for Information Professionals* (Stuart, 2016).

The RDF triple is the basic unit of the semantic web, based around the idea that all data can be encoded in the form of subject-predicate-object triples that can be expressed with the basic RDF vocabulary. A simple triple might express the idea that:

<David><Hates><Apple>

Although these concepts could be expressed in free text, linked data is 'the Semantic Web done right' (Heath, 2009), and emphasises the importance of having URIs to identify things, that these URIs are dereferenceable (can be looked up online) and link to other things. This allows triples to build on concepts that have already been defined elsewhere, and data to become part of an integrated web of data. Each of the three concepts could be expressed with URIs that already exist online:

- David (the author of this book) is already represented in the British National Bibliography <http://bnb.data.bl.uk/id/person/StuartDavid%28DavidPatrick%29>.
- Hates could be replaced by not_interested_in from the Weighted Interests Vocabulary <http://purl.org/ontology/wi/core#not_interested_in>.
- Apple (the technology company) is one of many entities with a Wikipedia page, which means it also exists as part of DBpedia, the structured content of Wikipedia published as linked data <http://dbpedia.org/resource/Apple_Inc.>.

The URIs have an important role in distinguishing between the page and the concept. The URIs above for David and Apple can be entered into a browser window and the relevant record returned. However, when resource URIs are requested the server responds with a *303 see other* status code, redirecting the client to the URI of the page associated with the requested resource:

<http://bnb.data.bl.uk/id/person/StuartDavid%28DavidPatrick%29>

becomes

<http://bnb.data.bl.uk/doc/person/StuartDavid%28DavidPatrick%29>,

and

<http://dbpedia.org/resource/Apple_Inc.>

becomes

<http://dbpedia.org/page/Apple_Inc.>.

The alternative, hash rather than slash, approach uses a hash fragment at the end of a URI to distinguish between a concept and a page, typically #this.

There are various ways for each of these triples to be serialised, each of which has their own particular advantages and disadvantages. These are only discussed briefly here, with just the one JSON-LD example provided. Different triple stores (databases purpose-built for RDF triples) and other semantic web tools can generally work with multiple different serialisations, and there are several tools for translating RDF from one serialisation to another: the online RDF Translator (http://rdf-translator.appspot.com) or command line tools such as RDF2RDF (www.l3s.de/~minack/rdf2rdf/) and Apache Jena Java framework rdfcat package (https://jena.apache.org).

The RDF/XML serialisation is the longest established of the serialisations and is compatible with most semantic web tools, but is not particularly human-friendly; more human-friendly serialisations have become more popular in recent years. The N-Triples serialisation is very simple for a human to understand, with the subject, predicate and object written in full as a single line of text, but extremely verbose with a lot of repetition within similar URLs. Turtle is like N-Triples, and is similarly human-friendly, but is far less verbose as it allows compact URIs and nested references, and importantly the Turtle syntax forms the basis of the RDF query language SPARQL. In 2014 Turtle was described as the 'de facto' RDF serialisation (van Hooland and Verborgh, 2014, 210), although its popularity has probably since been surpassed by JavaScript Object Notation for Linked Data (JSON-LD).

JSON is an increasingly popular format for sharing data that is far faster to process than XML and is directly supported by JavaScript while remaining human readable (Nurseitov et al., 2009). JSON-LD is totally compatible with JSON and therefore data publishers can continue using existing tools and include JSON-LD in HyperText Mark-up Language (HTML) web pages, which has led to the suggestion that it may help with the wider adoption of semantic web technologies (Lanthaler and Gütl, 2012). The JSON-LD specification has been written with developers in mind, trying to break away from the perceived tendency of the RDF community to create specifications that are insular (Sporny, 2014). Many organisations have adopted JSON-LD, including Google Knowledge Graph Search API (https://github.com/json-ld/json-ld.org/wiki/Users-of-JSON-LD). In JSON-LD the <David><Hates> <Apple> triple could be written as:

```
{
 "@context": {
 "wi": "http://purl.org/ontology/wi/core#"
 },
 "@id": "http://bnb.data.bl.uk/id/person/StuartDavid%28DavidPatrick%29",
 "wi:not_interested_in": {
 "@id": "http://dbpedia.org/resource/Apple_Inc."
 }
}
```

Although linked data has been separated out from standalone files and APIs here, in reality the categories are not distinct. Linked data may be available via an API or a standalone file, or embedded into web pages. It is linked data because of the way it is structured, rather than the way it is retrieved.

Unstructured data

Structured data is generally easier to analyse than unstructured data, and in some instances it might be perverse to analyse unstructured data when similar structured data is already available. It is nonetheless important to recognise the vast amount of unstructured data that is increasingly available and the growing number of tools there are for analysing it.

Although a distinction has been made here between structured and unstructured data, in reality the distinction is far from clear, with the same data often including structured and unstructured data. For example, in a sample of Twitter comments including a particular term or hashtag, analysing from where in the world the comments originated uses highly structured data, but analysing the sentiment of the comments uses highly unstructured data.

The value of unstructured data is in its quantity and richness. It has been suggested that structured data only accounts for 5% of digital data that is available (Mayer-Schönberger and Cukier, 2013). The web provides an extensive corpus of text on any topic that may be of interest, from informal discussions of the mundane (e.g. reality TV on social media) to highly erudite works on scholarly subjects (e.g. academic books and articles). There may be barriers to its analysis, caused by the diffusion of works across the web, language of publication, commercial interests and legal impediments, but the texts are there for analysis and the value is increasingly recognised. In the UK the copyright exemption for text and data mining is designed to allow non-commercial researchers to copy works they have the right to read for computational analysis, without requiring additional permissions from the publisher (Intellectual Property Office, 2014). The 2017 report for the UK government called *Growing the Artificial Intelligence Industry in the UK* recognises the potential value to the economy from extending these rights to the commercial sector, and recommends 'the right to read is also the right to mine data' (Hall and Pesenti, 2017, 49) for published research.

The large quantity of unstructured data available can be analysed not only with an increasing range of machine learning and data mining tools and software libraries, but manually. This may be achieved on a larger scale with crowdsourcing platforms, or by an individual using qualitative software such as NVivo or the open source alternative R package for Qualitative Data Analysis (RQDA). The point is that there is ever more unstructured textual data available, and tools for turning it into increasingly structured data for analysis.

Growing quantities of images and video can be used for automated analysis, for example significant progress in recent years in AI and image recognition. Social network services like Facebook offer the opportunity for tag suggestions and friendships based on images (Kelion, 2018), advertising screens increasingly incorporate cameras for displaying targeted advertisements (Reynolds, 2017), and the police use facial recognition to match people on police 'watch lists' (Coleman, 2019). Unsurprisingly, people are not always happy to be identified so easily or, conversely, wrongly labelled. Access to ever larger quantities of unstructured data invariably comes at the cost of increasing ambiguity, especially where there are fewer learning examples, potentially marginalising already marginalised communities.

Text analysis and mining has many applications in the library, and is returned to in Chapter 7. Most information professionals are less likely to use image analysis, which is not discussed in this book at any length. Nonetheless it is important that library and information professionals are aware of the increased capabilities that are offered, and the implications of the decisions that they make: the smart advertising board the public library accepts on its premises to bolster the book budget may capture a host of data users do not want captured; the promotional image employed for social media marketing may lead to the identification of users who do not wish to be recognised. The ethical implications from AI are legion and information professionals must be on their guard.

Data sources

There has been an explosion in the amount of data that is available in recent years, for a number of converging and overlapping reasons:

- the web
- open data
- tools, sensors and the internet of things.

Each of these are considered in turn, along with bibliographic data, a set of resources from several organisations likely to be particularly pertinent to information professionals. Library and information professionals need to be able to find all the data that is increasingly available; this is explored in the section on open data.

The web

It is impossible to over-estimate the impact that the web has had on people's lives. Since the first web page was published in 1991 (http://info.cern.ch/hypertext/WWW/TheProject.html) the web has grown from being primarily a static set of documents to interactive services where we do our shopping, meet our partners, find new homes, and chat to our friends. This move online has created vast swathes of data by web users, some intentional, much of it not.

That some of our online actions create data is not unsurprising, it is often necessary. We do not expect to be able to order an item from an online retailer without letting them know what we want to buy, how we'll pay, and where and to whom they should send it. Of course the big online retailers collect far more data than that, building up extensive customer profiles. They not only track what you put in your shopping basket, but what you looked at, how long you lingered, what you searched for, and who you know.

As advertising networks span multiple platforms and websites, this data collection is increasingly joined up, and personalised adverts can follow you across the web. Look at pushchairs on one website and adverts for associated baby items can follow you elsewhere online. However, in an age when the potential of AI and bespoke recommendation services are widely lauded these adverts can often show the crudeness of the algorithms that are in place, lacking the context to make them truly useful.

The web is more and more mobile as people access the services and information they need on mobile devices. This not only increases the amount of data that is available, as we are able to access the web more often, but also enables our surfing habits to be combined with other information, such as location data. This is returned to in the section 'Tools, sensors and the internet of things', below.

These personalised services not only have implications for our privacy, but have led to the suggestion that we are increasingly living in filtered bubbles (Pariser, 2011). Recent studies have found that concerns about such filter bubbles may be exaggerated (Haim, Graefe and Brosius, 2018), but just because such filtering is not exhibited in mainstream news services today it does not mean it won't be in the future, while the implications of small preferences in a complex system are difficult to understand. As Schelling famously demonstrated with regards to racial segregation, small preferences can have unexpected outcomes (Schelling, 2006).

The GDPR, which came into force across the EU in May 2018, place limits on the data that can be captured and stored by organisations without the explicit consent of customers, and although the regulations might limit some of the more egregious gathering of data, it seems likely that in most cases web users merely accept whatever is required to access the services they want. Where a website is a significant communication channel, like Facebook, it is not really possible to opt out unless you want to make it much more difficult to communicate with friends, family and the groups you are part of. Although in 2018 there were many news stories about the misuse of Facebook data and concerns about the sharing of fake news there seems to have been little impact on its market dominance, with the number of users continuing to rise (BBC News, 2019a).

It is important to recognise the gap between reality and the individual as seen through the lens of the new technologies. Individuals who might be deemed anxious when studying their Google searches may differ considerably from confident individuals promoted on social media. While Google may be a confessional, allowing people to express their darkest thoughts, it skews towards the forbidden (Stephens-Davidowitz, 2018); we may see it as more truthful, but we should be wary of considering it to be an absolute truth.

Open data
The web is not only a source of data, but also a place for publishing data, and in recent years the amount of data that has been shared has grown significantly, driven by calls for increased robustness in science, greater transparency in government, and the commercial opportunities from businesses opening themselves up to new horizons.

The breadth of data sets now available is astounding, and in much the same way as you might expect someone somewhere to have written something on a topic you are interested in, increasingly you can expect someone somewhere to have published some relevant data of interest. A glimpse of the breadth of the data that is now available can be seen in some of the general lists and directories of public data sets. For example, Awesome Public Datasets (https://github.com/caesar0301/awesome-public-datasets) lists data sets for natural language processing and image processing, from the social sciences to the hard sciences, and from commercial, government and non-profit organisations. The open data question-and-answer community on Open Data Stack Exchange (https://opendata.stackexchange.com) shows the wide range of data available and the uses people want to put it to.

Beyond such 'awesome' public data sets there is the long tail of data sets increasingly being published in institutional and organisational repositories, as well as on personal websites. However, identifying a data set that is shared can be a bit like searching for a needle in a haystack, and although general data services are being developed, for example, Google Dataset Search (https://toolbox.google.com/datasetsearch), there is not a single one-stop shop for practical purposes, and nor should we expect there to be in the near future.

Scientific data
The scientific community, in its broadest sense, increasingly expects data and a wider range of other research outputs (e.g. computer code) to be made publicly available. It is an important part of ensuring the robustness of science and that the most value can be extracted for each research pound, euro or

dollar invested. As vast quantities of data are shared and made available, it also facilitates a new way of doing science, a so-called fourth paradigm of science using data-intensive computing (Bell, 2009). Other reasons for managing and publishing research data include: increasing the visibility of data, saving time, simplifying research life, preserving data, increasing research efficiency, meeting grant requirements and supporting open access (Si et al., 2015).

There has been a cultural change in recent years in attitudes to the sharing of data, with increased recognition of the need for data expertise across research groups (Donati and Woolston, 2017). The limitations of publishing data on paper have been transformed by the web, and although the lack of sharing data was described as the dirty secret of science (Borgman, 2012), and expected growth in research data services was not found in libraries (Tenopir et al., 2015), there are signs of change.

It is not enough for scientific data to be shared, it must be discoverable. A recent survey found the majority of researchers rated the importance of making their data discoverable highly (Stuart et al., 2018). Unfortunately data is not always discoverable: scientific data is only one of a great many different types of information vying for attention on the web, and often researchers don't have the time or skills necessary to make the data as discoverable as possible, ensuring it is in the most appropriate repository, accompanied by the necessary metadata and documentation.

There are three principal entry points for identifying scientific research data on the web: repositories, subject directories or library guides, and data search engines. This does not preclude the possibility of looking for data in a traditional web search engine (e.g. Google) or contacting researchers directly to enquire about access to their data. Although we have reached the stage where there is data available on practically every subject, we have not reached the stage where we can expect any specific data we want to be available. Similar to the information-centric approach to research (Thelwall, Wouters and Fry, 2008), the tools available inevitably facilitate a data-centric rather than a problem-centred approach to research, which raises questions about whether public funds are being used to fund the most important or simply the easiest research.

Repositories may be institutional, regional, subject specific or unrestricted, and in June 2019 the Registry of Research Data Repositories (https://www.re3data.org) had records for 2,346 different repositories. These range from the highly specific and specialised, for example the Brain Biodiversity Bank (https://msu.edu/~brains), to broad subject repositories, such as UK Data Archive (www.data-archive.ac.uk) for the social sciences and the humanities. General repositories such as Zenodo (https://zenodo.org) and Figshare (https://figshare.com) have few restrictions about the data that is being made publicly available.

Thousands of library guides have now been created as introductions for data resources at LibGuides Community (https://community.libguides.com). Some contain expansive catalogues of data resources that are coupled with consultative services (e.g. the Data and Statistical Services at Princeton University, https://dss.princeton.edu), although the futility of such services may be likened to early attempts at trying to index the web manually. They can only succeed at a very rough level of granulation.

Some data search engines have been developed for a finer level of indexing across repositories, for example, Elsevier's DataSearch (https://datasearch. elsevier.com) and DataONE (www.dataone.org). These search engines have APIs for interacting with their data, making them potential objects of study in their own right.

Government data

Governments have always been among the biggest collectors of data, bearing out the dictum that 'knowledge is power', and in recent years have faced calls for transparency into their activities and the data that has been collected. As is generally the case with these things, arguments for social progress are only given serious consideration when they are supported by financial arguments, and governments were responding to the idea that the data they were sitting on had financial value that was not being fully realised at a time of general austerity.

There are now examples of data repositories and data sets being published at every level of government. From small local government repositories (e.g. Data Mill North, https://datamillnorth.org from Leeds City Council), through state (e.g. Hawaii Open Data, https://data.hawaii.gov) and national repositories (e.g. Kenya Open Data, www.opendata.go.ke), to transnational repositories (e.g. EU Open Data Portal, https://open-data.europa.eu). In addition there are many intermediaries bringing data together in one place, for example Data.gov for US government data and Data.gov.uk for UK government data. Intermediaries that bring together disparate data include libraries and non-profit organisations. Chapel Hill Open Data (www.chapelhillopendata.org) is a public library service that brings together data from the Town of Chapel Hill, North Carolina Department of Transport, and the US Census. The San Diego Regional Data Library (www.sandiegodata.org) is worth mentioning, not only for its high-lighting of data, but for its publishing of the Jupyter notebooks for analysing the data. Jupyter (https://jupyter.org) is an open source project that enables the sharing of notebooks of live code and visualisations on the web. Jupyter notebooks are an important part of sharing code in an interactive manner, and the code examples throughout this book have also been made available as notebooks at https://github.com/dpstuart/jupyter. For more details see the section 'Jupyter notebooks' in Chapter 4.

Data challenge competitions have regularly been run to encourage the use of government data and make it more accessible. Nesta, a UK innovation foundation, ran a series of seven open data challenges on jobs, heritage and culture, food, housing, education, energy and environment, and crime and justice (www.nesta.org.uk/project/open-data-challenge-series). The Library of Congress has also had a congressional data challenge to 'analyze, interpret or share congressional data in user-friendly ways' (Zwaard, 2017). These competitions are often at a national level, reflecting the fact that the net must be cast fairly wide to gain sufficient interest and entries. New York can boast a number of innovative open data responses (https://opendata.cityofnewyork. us/projects), but many smaller cities are unlikely to have the same well of human resources, and may struggle to maintain interest. There is undoubtedly a role for libraries to be the hub of such activities, promoting data use and accessibility at a local level. As with any voluntary work, it is a fine line between interesting and empowering work for the public good and exploitation of the public.

A vast range of data is available under freedom of information (FoI) legislation. Since it came into force in the UK in 2005 this legislation has been used to reveal diverse information about government behaviour and decisions, from the cost of policing football matches to the MP's expenses (Rosenbaum, 2015), and certain types of information are now published rather than having to be requested. Those working in public or university libraries will already be aware of the long reach of FoI requests, and other examples are available at What Do They Know (https://www.whatdotheyknow.com/), a website where people can make and track their FoI requests. For example, at the time of writing it gives details on 54 requests that have been made of the British Library (www.whatdotheyknow.com/body/the_british_library), from requests about the money spent on external contractors to queries regarding the depositing of a specific book.

Businesses
As well as the vast quantities of data being gathered and collected in-house, businesses are under increasing pressure to be more transparent and benefit from the wisdom of the crowd.

Successful online retailers and social media services have long recognised the need to tap into the wisdom of the crowd, with harnessing collective intelligence and data as the next intel inside being two of the attributes of those successful second generation or 'Web 2.0' web services (O'Reilly,

2005). Online retailers such as Amazon and eBay, as well as social media services like Facebook, Twitter and Instagram, have opened up data APIs to enable new tools and software to be built around their core service. A side effect of these APIs is that they have enabled research to be carried out on public attitudes and behaviour. For example, Twitter data has been used to show how people's moods change at different times of day (Golder and Macy, 2011). Although as has already been mentioned, following the Cambridge Analytica scandal many social media companies have become more circumspect about the data that they share.

Other examples of publishing data to harness the wisdom of the crowd are more explicit, with innovation platforms emerging that allow businesses to pose problems for the public to solve (e.g. InnoCentive, www.innocentive. com). These may include the sharing of data associated with the particular problem.

Businesses are increasingly aware of people's growing interest in ethical consumerism, with customers concerned about a company's environmental impact, work place conditions and diversity, and business practices. Even if a company is not sharing information about themselves, it may be shared by government or other organisations. For example, in the UK the Government Equalities Office publishes data about the gender pay gap (https://data.gov.uk/dataset/gender-pay-gap); Open Corporates (https://opencorporates.com) publishes data about corporate structures and officers; and Sourcemap (https://open.sourcemap.com) publishes data about supply chains. Some organisations have taken steps to publicise their own data, using platforms such as CarbonCulture (https://platform.carbonculture.net/communities/jll/31/) to share data about energy consumption and Sourcemap to share 'official' supply chains (e.g. Reese's Peanut Butter Cups, https://open.sourcemap.com/maps/589e04f7c2a8cac86bda3e29).

Programmable Web (www.programmableweb.com) is a particularly useful source of information about some of the available data sources. It has been around many years, and at the time of writing lists over 21,000 different APIs. Questions about open data may be asked at the already mentioned Open Data Stack Exchange (https://opendata.stackexchange.com).

Galleries, libraries, archives and museums
Cultural heritage institutions provide access to various resources for reasons of education, enjoyment and insight, and many have been exploring ways of making their data available. This is not only a natural extension to the public access so many institutions already provide, but as many of the institutions are also research institutions, it is part of the wider move to a more open science.

Most cultural heritage institutions that have made data available have started with catalogue records, although increasingly these are not only program-matically accessible, but are associated with a range of digital objects. As of June 2019, the British Museum collection database had 2.3 million records available, of which over 1 million had one or more images (www. britishmuseum.org/research/collection_online/search.aspx). Similarly, the V&A claims it has published records for over 1.2 million objects and over 750,000 images (http://collections.vam.ac.uk). As well as catalogue records with images many richer data objects have been released. These include collections of digitised books and manuscripts (e.g. Digitised Books from the British Library, https://data.bl.uk/digbks), sound recordings (e.g. the Animal Sound Archive from the Museum für Naturkunde in Berlin, www. animalsoundarchive.org), film (e.g. Imperial War Museum Film, https://film.iwmcollections.org.uk) and 3D models (e.g. Sketchfab hosts 3D collections from several museums, including the British Museum, https://sketchfab.com/britishmuseum). Whereas once it was only the text files that were appropriate for computational analysis, now a host of tools are available for analysis of these richer types of content, and their number is only likely to grow with the increase in tools for capturing 2D and 3D images, and users' expectations about being able to interact with these images.

Much of this content is reused elsewhere, for example, Europeana (www.europeana.eu) brings together data from multiple partners into a collection of over 57 million objects. This is part of a move to seeing 'collections as data', a strategic approach to making collections available for computational analysis, and the subject of institutes (e.g. https://collectionsasdata.github.io) and symposiums (https://www. youtube.com/watch?v=OJWMHzgCu3c).

Many controlled vocabularies and ontologies have been published (e.g. the Linked Data Service of the Library of Congress, https://id.loc.gov), and some museums are publishing their event and exhibition data in a machine readable format (e.g. the Museum of Modern Art Exhibition and Staff Histories, https://github.com/MuseumofModernArt/exhibitions).

Tools, sensors and the internet of things

As well as the web allowing existing data to be shared, the growth in the quantity and specification of tools and sensors has led to a massive growth in data. The near-ubiquitous mobile phone is now a complex bundle of sensors; we have increasingly incorporated sensors in the physical environment with turnstiles and swipe cards; and if you know the type of sensor that you are looking for it is relatively simple to find it online (e.g. from RS Components or Farnell).

Smartphones are now equipped with a range of sensors as standard. For example, the bestselling phone in 2018, the iPhone X, includes a front camera, a back camera, an infrared camera, an ambient light sensor, a proximity sensor, a microphone, an accelerometer, a gyroscope and a barometer. It can connect with Wi-Fi, GPS, Bluetooth and near field communication, as well as the usual 2, 3, and 4G telecommunication signals, enabling the identification of geographic location and nearby devices. Some other mainstream high-end phones have been installed with magnetometers for compass bearings and temperature sensors (for ambient rather than internal temperatures). More specialised phones offer thermal imaging and air quality sensors. The rapid increase in the specification of these sensors can most clearly be seen in more detailed camera specification. Whereas the first camera phones had 0.1–1 megapixels, in 2018 Sony revealed its 48 megapixel smartphone sensor (Dent, 2018).

Increased technical specifications are not limited to smartphones. Computed tomography has grown from 57.6 KB in 1972 to 0.1–1 GB by 2010 (Kalender, 2011). In its first year 13 petabytes (10^{15} bytes) of data were collected from the Large Hadron Collider (Brumfiel, 2011), and in 2018 that is expected to rise to 50–70 petabytes (WLCG, 2018).

Sensors can be put in places they never were before to gather a host of specialist data. There are publicly available versions of smart footballs that promise to give you feedback on the power, spin and trajectory of your kick, and digital soles that promise not only to count your steps but also provide a 3D analysis of your stride. Sensors claim to give insights into your pet's mood by measuring its heartrate, and sensors for measuring the moisture level of your plants and the humidity of the air. Some sensors, such as air humidity sensors, probably have a wider application in the information sector than smart footballs or pet heartrate monitors, but it is important to recognise the potential for sensors to be applied in a host of different scenarios within libraries.

There has always been a need to capture certain data in the library to demonstrate value, whether counting the number of users, loans or queries at an enquiry desk, or gathering information from a customer satisfaction sensor. Technology increasingly offers the opportunity to extend the range of data, measuring use of particular areas of the library, using eye-tracking software to see how people interact with library home pages, or the environmental conditions of the library. The rise in makerspaces within libraries may provide the opportunity for collaboration between libraries and their users. Even where sensors may be difficult, or controversial to install, software has been developed to ease the process of data collection. For example, Suma (https://github.com/suma-project/Suma) is a toolkit for analysing the use of physical spaces in a library.

Bibliographic data

The web now provides a wealth of bibliographic data from many organisations with different priorities, and many of the examples in this book use the bibliographic data that is freely available online. Many libraries and other cultural heritage institutes are trying to broaden access to their collections, online retailers are trying to increase sales, citation databases (subscription and free) are expanding the ways you can access their data, and social network sites are trying to encourage users to engage with their services.

Catalogue data has been made available by many major national, university and special libraries. Notable library providers of bibliographic data include:

- collection metadata from the British Library (www.bl.uk/bibliographic/datafree.html)
- MARC Distribution Services of the Library of Congress (www.loc.gov/cds/products/marcDist.php)
- Harvard Library APIs and Datasets (https://library.harvard.edu/open-metadata).

Open Library (https://dev.openlibrary.org), an open editable catalogue from the Internet Archive, has the aim of one web page for every book ever published.

Associated with bibliographic data is growing interest in the relationships between works and their readers. Library loan data is particularly valuable; the University of Huddersfield increased the number of books that were borrowed by combining usage data with catalogue data to make recommendations (Kay et al., 2010), although there are limitations on how it can be shared. Even within an institution it may be difficult to extract loan information because of setting or software limitations (Renaud et al., 2015). Alternative sources for insights include the social network sites Goodreads (www.goodreads.com) and LibraryThing (www.librarything.com), which provide extensive APIs for interacting with their respective book and research article data.

There are ever more sources for citation data from more open sources. Google Scholar (https://scholar.google.co.uk) has made citation data available to a wider range of users than subscription citation services, although the amount of data that is available programmatically through tools such as Publish or Perish (https://harzing.com/resources/publish-or-perish) is quite limited. More open alternative services such as OpenCitations (http://opencitations.net), CiteSeerX (http://citeseerx.ist.psu.edu) or Microsoft Academic (https://academic.microsoft.com) provide greater computational access to their data, but they are not currently as extensive or as high quality as the subscription services. Although there is growing interest in open citations, the gap in the openness of current bibliometrics and the openness that is necessary for the most robust and insightful evaluative and relational bibliometrics possible is still significant (Stuart, 2018).

The outputs of scholarly publishing – books, articles and the citations between them – do not exist in isolation, and there has been increased interest in understanding the relationship between scholarly outputs and the wider research environment. The web provides a source for capturing some of this information and a medium for sharing it.

Altmetrics is the use of the structured nature of social media technologies to establish alternative filters and indicators of research impact (Priem et al., 2010). The term may be used and widened to include the filtering and impact of non-traditional forms of output, including computer code and data sets (Stuart, 2014). Open Syllabus (http://opensyllabus.org) shares data on 6 million syllabi from about 6,000 institutions. Altmetric (www.altmetric.com) brings together data from social media, online reference managers, Open Syllabus and other sources, and currently offers an API that is free to academic researchers. SciGraph (https://scigraph.springernature.com) provides a linked data set of the scholarly universe that is not only restricted to publications, but puts publications in the context of research grants. The Lens (www.lens.org) combines scholarly and patent search and analysis.

Data licences

Although this is not a book on intellectual property rights (IPR), it would be remiss to write a book on data science without at least a brief word on IPR and the wider legal framework within which analysis is taking place. Information professionals find there are restrictions in what data publishers and the law allow, and what may be considered ethical behaviour.

There are many data licences as well as bespoke terms and conditions restricting the way publicly available data may be reused. These range from the extremely open to the extremely restrictive. Harvard University Library, for example, publishes its metadata under a Creative Commons Zero licence. At the other end of the continuum the social cataloguing site Goodreads provides its API with a number of bespoke restrictions (https://www.goodreads.com/api), limiting the value of an extremely rich data set. Not only does the prohibition on the use of the data in commercial products potentially restrict its adoption by certain groups, but the restriction on storing the information beyond 24 hours is likely to limit its value to researchers (https://www.goodreads.com/api/terms). Although standardised data licences simplify the process of creating a licence and reusing the data, the many licences that have been applied can nonetheless cause confusion and conflict where multiple data sources are used with different licences (Ball, 2014), or if the data provider has different licences for different data sets.

Such licences also work in the wider legal framework. And even if you own the data, there may be restrictions on how you can use it, especially with regards to personal data following the introduction of the GDPR. Most people's experience of the GDPR occurs when we are required to agree with increasingly complicated policies whenever we visit a new website, but the GDPR have more practical implications for data scientists. Dinsmore (2017) identifies three: it limits data processing and consumer profiling; it creates a 'right to an explanation' when used for automated decision making; and it holds firms accountable for automated decisions that result in bias and discrimination. The full implications of the GDPR are still being realised as the legislation meets judicial interpretation and the state of the art in AI and machine learning. The Information Commissioner's Office (2017) notes three implications from a fairness perspective: big data analytics has the potential to have an intrusive effect on individuals; organisations must consider whether people might reasonably expect their data to be used in big data applications; and state of the art machine learning can make it difficult to be transparent about the processing of personal data.

Many large organisations have instituted GDPR training to ensure staff do not fall foul of GDPR legislation, but it is important to remember that even if something is legal, it doesn't necessarily mean it is ethical. Libraries are among some of the most trusted institutions, partly because they adhere to codes of ethics that go above and beyond the legal requirements (Berman, 2018). Library users trust libraries with their data, data about the resources accessed as well as personal details, and though data science offers the opportunity for new insights and services, it must not come at a loss of the trust which librarians currently hold.

3

The process of data science

Data science is the process by which insights may be gleaned from the data that is available. This chapter considers some of the different models that have been proposed for the data science process, and provides a five-stage procedure that can be applied by information professionals:

- Frame the problem
- Collect data
- Transform and clean data
- Analyse data
- Visualise and communicate data.

As is discussed below, such a model is necessarily an oversimplification, but nonetheless provides a framework for discussing some of the steps common to many data science studies in the chapters that follow: Chapter 4 considers some of the tools available for each of these stages, before chapters 5, 6 and 7 consider some of the main data analysis techniques more closely.

This chapter starts by discussing the construction of the five-stage procedure, its advantages and (many) limitations.

Modelling the data science process

It is important to recognise that no model captures the myriad of different studies that fall under the banner of 'data science'. Some start with a question, but others start with the data, the analysis or even a visualisation. So why bother to model the data science process? Primarily to take the complexity of the information ecosystem, which can quickly become overwhelming with its variety of data, tools and questions, and encapsulate the process so that it can be considered more holistically.

There are different ways that the data science process can be modelled. Hayashi (1996), for example, models data science as a three step process: design, collection, analysis. Springboard (2016) breaks down the collection and analysis stages further, reflecting the inevitable need to clean the data that is collected and the different objectives of exploratory and in-depth analysis. Marr (2015) and Springboard (2016) recognise the importance of communicating the findings. Data science is not about idle insights, it is about being able to turn those insights into actions. Table 3.1 summarises these three models of the data science process.

Table 3.1 *Models of the data science process*

Hayashi (1996)	Marr (2015)	Springboard (2016)
1 Design for data	1 Strategy	1 Frame the problem
2 Collect data	2 Measure	2 Collect the raw data needed for your problem
		3 Process the data for analysis
3 Analyse data	3 Analyse	4 Explore the data
		5 Perform in-depth analysis
	4 Report	6 Communicate the results of the analysis
	5 Transform	

However the process is modelled, it is important to recognise that rather than comprising distinct steps the whole process is iterative, and it is often necessary to return to an earlier step. An initial framing of the problem may need to be reappraised in response to the realities of data collection (e.g. the cost of obtaining the data may turn out to be prohibitively expensive). Data transformation and cleaning may turn out to be so arduous that an alternative data source must be found. Preliminary data analysis may find the data cannot provide the insights required and it is necessary to return to the data collection stage. Alternatively the inability of data to provide insights may only become apparent after the data has been visualised. There is a need for data scientists to be agile, always willing to revisit an earlier stage, reassess the data sources or research tools they are using. Alternatively, information professionals may find themselves starting at any of the various stages in the cycle as they collaborate with researchers who have already begun the cycle.

The rest of this chapter considers the data science process according to the five-stage process shown in Figure 3.1 opposite: frame the problem, collect data, transform and clean data, analyse data, and visualise and communicate data. The steps have been shown in a loop to emphasise the ongoing process of data science, with the results of one study potentially helping with the framing of new questions. As has already been mentioned, at any stage it may be necessary to return to a previous stage. The same stage may be repeated multiple times, and it is because the process is iterative that the analysis section has not been divided between exploratory and in-depth

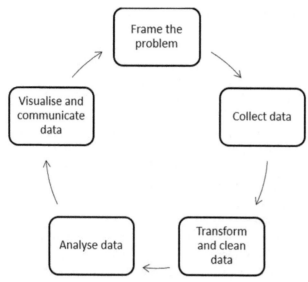

Figure 3.1 *The five-stage process of data science*

analysis. That would suggest an exactness that is in truth lacking from any such model. At the same time, although data visualisation has been coupled with communication, as it is such an important part of the communication stage, it could just as easily have been coupled with (or even before) data analysis. For example, you may need to know the distribution of data to use a particular statistical test, and this may be most easily done with a histogram. 'Transform' is not explicitly in the model because often transformation of the system or organisation is beyond the influence of information professionals, but they can change the questions they ask and frame next.

The rest of the chapter addresses the model in more detail. Although it may occasionally suggest definitive stages or an order, in reality there is no such thing.

Frame the problem

Data science starts with framing the problem: explicitly stating the problem, establishing the boundaries, and identifying an initial strategy to approach it. As Buckley Owen (2017, 2) has said of the traditional research desk enquiry, 'people almost never ask the question to which they really want to know the answer', and the same is true with data science where problems are often stated ambiguously (Springboard, 2016). The task of information professionals as data scientists is to take vague and misdirected questions and make them more concrete, and help establish a plan of action for operationalising the question.

Information professionals are typically recommended to respond to an initial reference desk enquiry by asking a question to gain a fuller understanding of the query: who?, what?, when?, where?, why?, how? (Buckley Owen, 2017). Similar questions may be asked of a data science problem, whether it appears at the reference desk or emerges from within the library itself. For example, the question 'How can I use the library's data to improve library performance?' asks what is, or can be, included in a library's data and how we judge a library's performance. Is a library's data limited to internal data generated by the library, or can external data the library has access to be included? Does the data have to be available now, or is it something that can be gathered over time? How is library performance to be measured? Millions of pounds could easily be saved by closing the library down, although most would agree that such a crude metric of performance would be wholly useless.

'Why?' questions are particularly important when responding to people from outside the information profession who may have an unsophisticated idea about the tools or insights available from different data sources. The person with the bibliometric enquiry 'Which are the most highly cited research groups in my field?' may be interested in the answer because they want to spot emerging research areas, compare the impact factors of different groups, or simply be looking for a new job. Understanding why he or she asked the question may suggest more pertinent lateral approaches: are the formal institutionalised research groups as important as the informal invisible colleges reflected in publications or online social networks? How should the field be operationalised? What boundaries and types of institution should be included?

Such questions must necessarily be handled sensitively, because of the possible nature of the topic, and because of the power imbalance caused by the knowledge gap between the enquirer and information professional. Partlo (2010) highlights the important role of teaching in the work of the data librarian, not just meeting the library user at the level they are at. This may be particularly true of the undergraduate student, but while it has been suggested that established researchers are aware of the data sets and providers available in their field (Rice and Southall, 2017) it seems far more likely that they suffer from huge gaps in knowledge too, especially in those areas where traditionally there has not been such a technical focus. For example, in the humanities there has been growing interest in computational methods such as distant reading (Moretti, 2013), the idea that new insights may be gathered about works by analysing patterns across a whole corpus rather than just close reading of a single work in isolation (Jänicke et al., 2015). The tools and resources necessary for such analysis differ significantly from the close reading that many researchers in the humanities would have been trained in. Although a new generation may be coming through with a wider range of digital skills, we should be wary of presuming too much.

Of all the questions that may be asked of a data science problem, one of the most important is 'What are the resources available?' The framing of any problem is inevitably restricted by the resources available, and in the information profession the resources are typically limited. While there may seemingly be endless supplies of relevant data available, the ability to use it is restricted according to data costs, and human and computational resources:

- *Data costs*: We are living in an age when a lot of data is available for free, especially library data, but there is still a lot of data that costs money, especially when it is used for commercial purposes. It is possible that the data required has not been captured yet, and there are costs involved with collecting it.
- *Human resources*: People are restricted by the number of hours they have available and their skill set. If someone only has a couple of hours to find an answer to a problem and their only experience of data analysis revolves around spreadsheets, there's probably little point in pointing them in the direction of an API for JSON records.
- *Computational resources*: While computing power is increasingly cheap, analysis of certain massive data sets can still be beyond the capabilities of a single desktop PC. Developments in cloud computing offer a cheaper alternative to establishing your own data centre, but cheaper is not free, and there are additional computer skill requirements.

Without an initial plan of action to act as a guide, it is very easy to fall into a rabbit hole of exploring unusual and enticing data sets and queries; it may indeed be the case that there is a correlation between the consumption of baked beans and a library's circulation figures, but it's probably not the best use of limited resources to investigate it. At this stage the plan of action is only a guide, and as the old military adage states, 'No plan survives contact with the enemy.' Unexpected data sources may appear, simple solutions may turn out to be more complicated than expected, and the problem itself may be refined to something more specific.

It may be that information professionals are only involved in the early stages of the data science problem, helping to frame the problem and identify data resources at the enquiry desk before the researcher goes off and does their work elsewhere. But as long as they are involved in the process it is necessary that they are willing to take an iterative approach and return to previous stages as often as is required.

Sometimes in data science you are not starting with a problem, but rather a data set. Data discovery is exploring data with no particular agenda or questions (Marr, 2015), similar to the information-centric approach to information science (Thelwall, Wouters and Fry, 2008). In a world of restricted library budgets and a need to demonstrate a return on investment, there is often little space for unrestricted exploration of data sets, but it is important to recognise that while it is not necessary to have a fully articulated problem, although without one you may be forced to explore the data in your own time.

Collect data

After framing the problem it is necessary to collect the data, and the complexity of this stage may sit anywhere on the continuum from extremely simple to extremely complicated. At the simple end of the spectrum, if you are aware of the appropriate data set, and it has already been collected and shared, then the process of collecting data may be as simple as visiting the appropriate web page and clicking on a 'download' button. At the more complicated end of the spectrum an extensive data search may prove fruitless, and you are required to collect the data yourself, either deploying sensors, writing programs to scrape the web, or firing off hundreds of FoI requests.

The huge variety of data types and sources has already been discussed in Chapter 2, and there is little benefit in providing an extensive list of instructions for each type. There are some general points about data collection to keep in mind, however, which are discussed below.

Data search is not as developed as document search

There is not currently the same infrastructure available to identify data as there is for documents. Although new services are improving the identification of data and data repositories, part of the problem is intrinsic to data itself, which often lacks the advantages of rich text for searching. The exact data you need may be sitting in a simple Excel file, but without someone creating the metadata necessary, discovery could be limited to the half dozen keywords used in the column headings.

Data is fragmented

Books and articles weave together narratives, drawing together multiple sources into a coherent whole through references. In comparison, data is often fragmented with multiple related data sets spread across multiple sites, with no, or minimal, links between the sets.

Not all data is online

As librarians must continually reiterate, not everything is online, and this is as true of data as the published word, if not more so. The step from preparing a scholarly document to placing it in an online repository is a small one, whereas the time needed to make data suitable for a wider audience is likely to be far larger, especially if it is to be accompanied by the documentation necessary for it to be practically useful. Until data and non-traditional research outputs are valued as highly as journal articles or monographs, its online availability and findability continues to lag behind.

Not all data is available now

There is a lot of data that has not been captured yet. While the data set you are looking for might not be available, the infrastructure to collect the data might be. For example, there are often differences in data for operational systems and data for analysis, with transactional systems often deleting data when transactional data is no longer required (Nicholson, 2006b). In Renaud et al.'s (2015) mining of integrated library system data, personal information wasn't retained with the historical circulation data in the integrated library system, so a snapshot of checked-out items was taken weekly, leading to the duplication of entries as many items are checked out for over a week. Data warehousing, collecting vast quantities of data just in case it is needed in the future, may provide a partial solution for data with a high probability of future use, but there is always unexpected data that has not been captured.

Data varies in quality and authority

It seems more likely that someone will deliberately misquote the president of the US than create fake data about a city's morgue of frozen animals, but it is nonetheless important that reasonable and appropriate steps are taken to ensure the legitimacy of the data that is being used. Is the source authoritative and has it got a particular agenda? An animal rights campaign group may be an authority on animal cruelty, but you might be tempted to take its figures on cruelty with a pinch of salt.

Data exists in a wider legal and ethical framework

As has already been mentioned, whether using your organisation's data or data from the web, it is important to consider the legal and ethical implications of dealing with data. The GDPR incorporate restrictions on how data gathered for one purpose can be used in another and data from external sources may be subject to copyright and licensing restrictions, even if it is freely accessible online. It is important to take appropriate steps to ensure that the person sharing data has the right to share it.

Know when to stop

There are always additional data sets that could provide more insights; one data set quickly leads to another. For example, Renaud et al. (2015) compared library use data with students' academic achievement, but recognised the potential of other data sets: student organisation participation, and use of tutoring, counselling or advisory services. As more data is captured there are ever more ways it can be combined and analysed, but at some point it is necessary to stop and work with what you have.

Transform and clean data

Even if the data is available right now, unless it happens to be in a data warehouse that you have designed and is waiting to be queried, it probably isn't in the format you want, and even if it is it will require some level of cleaning. The process of transforming the raw data you have access to into something that is suitable for data analysis is generally known as data wrangling or data munging, and broadly consists of two parts: data transformation and cleaning.

Data transformation is the process of converting data from one format or structure to another. Typically this is for one of two reasons: either the data is in an unwanted file format, or it adheres to an unwanted metadata schema.

Generally it is easier to convert from one file format to another as software can often import from and export into many formats. For example, as well as being able to open current and historic Excel documents, Microsoft Excel can be used to import CSVs, HTML tables and Access tables, as well as connecting with various other databases and APIs. It is important to be aware of structural issues when converting between file formats, however; for example, a network graph or an XML hierarchy may not translate to a single table. Alternatively the software may include idiosyncrasies in the transformation, for example ignoring certain attributes, and it is therefore always important to check that records have transformed as expected. Of course, away from the well-known file formats, there is a long tail of more obscure formats that may be arrived at only after multiple transformations with different software or a bespoke bit of code. As a general rule, open standards are preferable and proprietary ones to be avoided.

Crosswalking

Even if the data is in the right file format, or has been easily transformed into the right file format, it does not necessarily adhere to the metadata schema required. Specific data analysis software may require the data to adhere to a particular schema, or multiple sources may have data adhering to different schemas which prevents analysis and comparison. A crosswalk is a field-to-field mapping between metadata schemas based on the semantics of the fields (Gartner, 2016); although simple in theory, a crosswalk can often be complicated in practice and it inevitably lowers the quality of the metadata overall. Even where the fields are similar, there are often subtle differences in the meanings associated with the terms, and more often it requires data in the highly specific elements to be crosswalked to broader elements. Crosswalks from the general to the specific are only possible with a lot of additional work.

Table 3.2 shows the different types of MAchine-Readable Cataloging (MARC) name fields being reduced to the single element 'contributor' when crosswalked from MARC to Dublin Core (Library of Congress, 2008b), while crosswalking back from Dublin Core to MARC (Library of Congress, 2008a) necessarily uses the vaguest of the associated MARC fields. Information has been lost about whether it is a main or added entry, and the type of name, even before the subfield codes are considered, which may include titles, dates and affiliations associated with a name.

Table 3.2 A crosswalk from MARC to Dublin Core and back

MARC field	Dublin Core element	MARC field
100: Main entry – Personal name	Contributor	720: Added entry – Uncontrolled
110: Main entry – Corporate name	Contributor	720: Added entry – Uncontrolled name
111: Main entry – Meeting name	Contributor	720: Added entry – Uncontrolled name
700: Added entry – Personal name	Contributor	720: Added entry – Uncontrolled name
710: Added entry – Corporate name	Contributor	720: Added entry – Uncontrolled name
711: Added entry – Meeting name	Contributor	720: Added entry – Uncontrolled name
720: Added entry – Uncontrolled name	Contributor	720: Added entry – Uncontrolled name

Information professionals do not want to eliminate such loss of information, but reduce it as far as reasonably possible. Too cavalier an approach and highly specific elements are left rattling around in highly general categories; an overly cautious approach to data loss and highly idiosyncratic bespoke schemas emerge that will never be used again (an accusation that can often be levelled at the digital humanities community).

Data linkage

Whereas crosswalking can lead to ill-fitting data, data linkage can introduce absolute errors. Data linkage is the process whereby separate data sets are joined. Where unique identifiers are shared between data sets (for example with ISBNs) then false matches only occur when there are errors in the original data sets, whereas without shared identifiers it is necessary to take probabilistic or deterministic approaches to data matching. It has been suggested, however, that linkage error can disproportionately affect disadvantaged groups (Gilbert et al., 2018).

Even if the data happens to be in the file format that you want, and adheres to the metadata schema that you require, it is nonetheless probably filled with errors. All data is invariably dirty data. Typical errors include missing values, corrupted values, time-zone differences and data range errors (Springboard, 2016), with additional problems likely to occur when combining multiple data sets. Two data sets may use different units of measurements or different date systems. Even in the information profession, which prides itself on establishing standards, there are often irregularities, and as standards change over time, so inconsistencies in the catalogue emerge. Data may also simply be badly formed. For example, RDF/XML is a notoriously unfriendly format, and numerous examples can be found online that fail RDF validation tests.

As the old computer science adage states: garbage in, garbage out. Unless steps are taken to clean the data properly, data analysis can be built on extremely weak foundations, and unfortunately surveys find data cleaning to be the most time consuming (and least enjoyable) part of the data science process (Press, 2016). Estimates of how much time is spent on a data cleaning process are as high as 80%.

Analyse data

As has already been mentioned, the data science process is highly iterative. Any of the stages may need to be repeated multiple times, or abandoned in favour of an earlier stage. This is most apparent at the data analysis stage, where the data inevitably needs to be probed and explored multiple times. Some have divided this into two stages: explore the data and analyse it in depth (Springboard, 2016), but even this further breakdown fails to express its true iterative nature, or the multiple times it may be necessary to analyse data: 'It is this process of iterative queries and cyclical review of the data that makes data mining such a powerful assessment tool' (Renaud et al., 2015, 358).

It is often only when you begin to probe data that its potential and idiosyncrasies start to emerge, but one must be careful when approaching this iterative process. As we explore large data sets piecemeal, with every additional test it becomes increasingly likely that we will find a correlation through the brute force of the number of queries that have been made rather than the power of deduction.

The traditional approach to this problem is to use the Bonferroni correction, dividing the p-value you require by the number of tests that you apply. For example, if you wish to achieve a significant p-value ($p<0.05$), but are testing 100 correlations in the data set, any of those correlations would have to achieve a far lower p-value ($p<0.0005$) to be considered significant. If you are running an extremely large number of tests on data, it can become extremely difficult for any correlation to be found to be significant, leading to a lot of false negatives. This has led to increased use of the Benjamini-Hochberg procedure, especially in the exploratory phase where positive results are then further explored afterwards. The p-values of the tests applied to a data set are ranked in order, and the Benjamini-Hochberg critical value is calculated for each one by dividing the p-value rank by the total number of tests and multiplying the result by the decided on false discovery rate. The largest p-value where p is less than the Benjamini-Hochberg critical value is considered significant, as are any ones that have a lower p-value.

Many approaches may be taken to data analysis, although within data science we are primarily considering those types of data analysis that have been enabled through the proliferation of computer hardware and software that enable analysis at speeds and scales, and generally with a consistency, that would not have been possible before. For example, sentiment analysis of texts would have always been possible, but the time it would take a researcher to classify a million comments would have made such a task prohibitive (without some sort of distribution of the task). Consistency is notoriously difficult to achieve between classifiers, and even for the same classifier over time. While data science methods can be applied consistently, that doesn't mean the same results are always achieved; variations in the data point that is used to start calculations may have a significant impact on the outcomes.

Data mining may be categorised into four types: association, classification, clustering and regression (Siguenza-Guzman et al., 2015). Each applies equally to the data analysis step of the data science process, and of these classification and regression models are most often used in a library setting

(Siguenza-Guzman et al., 2015). Classification attempts to discover predictive patterns by classifying records into predefined categories, whereas clustering is used to uncover unanticipated trends without predefined clusters. This distinction between predefined and undefined categorisation, and the associated supervised and unsupervised learning, are addressed in Chapter 5, 'Clustering and social network analysis', and the section on machine learning in Chapter 7, 'Text analysis and mining'. Regression makes predictions on existing data points, and is discussed in Chapter 6, 'Predictions and forecasts'.

Visualise and communicate data

The effective communication of data science results is an important part of persuading people of the veracity of the findings. There is now considerable visualisation functionality in desktop software (such as Microsoft Office), as well as specialised visualisation software and programming libraries. It is possible to generate a host of graphics with a few clicks of a button, which while impressive are virtually meaningless or, worse, misleading. Just because something can be done, does not mean it should be. In the same way that most of us learn to be sparing with the number of fonts and colours we use in a word-processing document, so we need to learn to be sensible with the visualisations that we choose.

We have all come across unengaging, impenetrable and misleading visualisations, and as the tools for creating them have become more widespread, most of us have probably created quite a few too. There is increasing recognition of the problem of bad visualisations, infographics and the ubiquitous 'death by PowerPoint', and many books and blogs dedicated to improving their quality, highlighting some of the most egregious errors, and showing the potential of good visualisations. Importantly these books and blogs are not only aimed at graphic designers, but the increasingly wide range of professionals who are expected to produce their own visualisations. Some are listed here:

- *Storytelling with Data* (Nussbaumer Knaflic, 2015) (www.storytellingwithdata.com)
- *The Truthful Art* (Cairo, 2016) (www.thefunctionalart.com)
- *Information is Beautiful* (McCandless, 2012) (https://informationisbeautiful.net)
- *Visual Insights* (Börner and Polley, 2014) (https://sci2.cns.iu.edu).

A full exploration of the types of visualisation and what they should and shouldn't include is beyond the scope of this book (and its author), but it is important to be aware of the range of visualisations available and some of the worst errors.

Börner and Polley (2014, 19) distinguish between charts, tables, graphs, geospatial maps and network graphs. Charts are visualisations without an inherent reference system, such as pie charts and word clouds. Tables can be visualisations, enabling the inclusion of colouring, graphics and hierarchies. Graphs such as scatter plots and bar graphs are widely used for displaying data. Geospatial maps use a geographic co-ordinate system to display data. Network graphs show data as a collection of connected nodes, for example in a taxonomic hierarchy or a co-authorship network. Some of the tools available for each of these chart types are explored in Chapter 4, 'Tools for data analysis'. Network graphs are discussed in Chapter 5, 'Clustering and social network analysis', graphs for forecasting in Chapter 6, 'Predictions and forecasts', and graphs for text analysis in Chapter 7 'Text analysis and mining'.

As increasingly complex visualisations have become widely available, there has been growing recognition of the importance of adhering to certain principles in their adoption. Waltman (2017) has suggested six principles of scientometric visualisation, which have been suggested as the basis for responsible visualisation more generally (Waltman, 2018):

1 Acknowledge different uses of visualisations.
2 Adjust visualisations to the mode of presentation.
3 Balance technical sophistication with transparency.
4 Recognise that visualisations are often simplifications.
5 Combine visualisations with other evidence.
6 Test sensitivity of visualisations to methodological choices.

Here discussion of visualisations is limited to three points: they should be truthful; they should be clear; they should be useful.

Visualisations should be truthful

Visualisations help tell a story, and some tell a story better than others, but that does not give you carte blanche to manipulate the data beyond all recognition. For example, during local elections in the UK there are often misleading graphs on leaflets. The size of the bars on graphs rarely reflect the figures they represent but more often the 'two horse race' that the political party wants it to be perceived as, and if this can only be achieved by including data from a totally different type of election with different boundaries, or at a different level of aggregation, then so be it.

With more complex visualisations, the need for honesty reflects Waltman's third principle, the need for methodological transparency. Processing data inevitably involves a lot of methodological choices in analysis and visualisation. For example, the same network graph can look extremely different depending on which algorithm is used, which point an algorithm is applied to first, or which features are differentiated. Figure 3.2 shows the same data as four different network graphs. Although the underlying data is the same for each graph, the largest clique is far more easily discernible in the Kamada-Kawai layout where the clique is a different colour (bottom right) than when the nodes are placed randomly (top left), in a circle (top right), or even using the Kamada-Kawai algorithm without different colours (bottom left). The Kamada-Kawai algorithm is only one of many different algorithms that may be used to determine the position of the nodes.

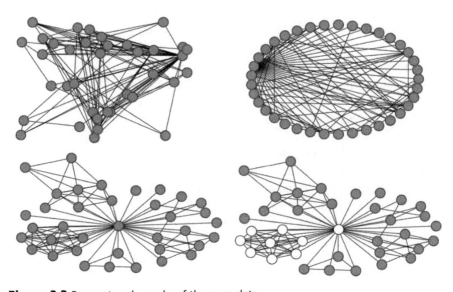

Figure 3.2 *Four network graphs of the same data*

Visualisation should be clear

Second, visualisation should be clear. Clear may mean different things in different situations, depending on the purpose and mode of presentation (Waltman's first and second principles). The visualisation that gains a person's attention is not necessarily the best for conveying quantitative information. For example, Xia and Wang (2014) use tag-clouding as a way of visualising the weighting of terms in a set of data librarian job adverts. While a tag cloud may provide insights into the dominance of certain terms, it's not necessarily the most robust way to identify terms as the basis of a quantitative academic paper. Similarly, although a static image of a visualisation may be considered sufficiently clear when published in a journal article, that same data may be better represented on the web with an interactive visualisation.

One of the best ways of making the results of data science clear is by enabling the data and code to be engaged with, and this is increasingly being embraced with the move towards open access and open code. The open source project Jupyter (https://jupyter.org) enables notebooks of live code and visualisations to be shared on the web, and one analysis on GitHub in September 2018 found more than 2.5 million public Jupyter notebooks (Perkel, 2018). See the section 'Programming for data science' in Chapter 4.

While the potential for producing ever larger and more complex data sets to create intricate and confusing visualisations is obvious, it should be noted that even the humble (and widespread) pie chart can cause confusion. As Nussbaumer Knaflic points out, people are not good at ascribing quantitative values to areas, or as she puts it more succinctly: 'Pie charts are evil' (Nussbaumer Knaflic, 2015, 61). Despite the shortcomings of our human visual perception, as most people are familiar with geographic regions of the world, geospatial graphs can be a particularly useful way to visualise data. Even cartograms, where the sizes of respective countries have been adjusted to reflect some particular aspect that needs emphasising, work better with significant global differences rather than small local differences (Figure 3.3).

Figure 3.3 *Cartogram of Europe with countries resized according to the number of Wikipedia page views*

Visualisations should be useful

Finally, and most importantly, visualisations should be useful. Visualisations in data science are a key part of helping people navigate data, generate hypotheses, understand the relationships between different facets, and communicate those findings to a wider audience. But while there are a lot of uses for visualisations, every visualisation is not necessarily useful.

Frame a new problem

Information professionals may be limited in their freedom to frame new problems continuously, especially where they are primarily providing data science support as a service in a library. But even where the problems addressed are unconnected and isolated, there is still the opportunity for them to feed back recommendations for future problems, and to build on their growing data science knowledge. If information professionals are to frame new problems in light of the experience and knowledge they have acquired during previous data explorations, and if this knowledge is not to be lost, then it must be captured.

As will become clear throughout this book, there is a vast array of data, methods and tools available for data scientists, but it is unrealistic to expect any individual to keep track of all the resources they use, let alone come across, without external aids. Detailed notes on the resources used and discounted, and how they were handled, will invariably help with applying the most appropriate tools and methods in future investigations. There is no single right way to capture a growing knowledge of data science resources and experiences – it may take the form of a blog, a Google Doc, Microsoft OneNote, Jupyter notebooks, or even an old fashioned paper notebook. It is more important that you find a method that you are comfortable with and fits into your working practice than one that ticks certain boxes. While the idea of a laboratory notebook may be new to many in the information profession, there is a lot of experience from the scientific community to build on (Pain, 2019).

4

Tools for data analysis

The laboratory equipment of data scientists is not test tubes and microscopes, but the set of software they install on their laptop or desktop. There are ever more tools available for budding data scientists, far too many to mention in a single chapter, and more appear all the time. Following a short discussion on the problem of data scientists finding the tools they need, the rest of this chapter is split into two parts, looking at software applications and programming tools available for data science.

Novice data scientists who have little or no programming experience are likely to choose pre-packaged software when analysing data. Several data science applications are designed to enable data collection, cleaning, analysis and visualisation for non-programmers, and some notable examples are discussed in this chapter according to where they appear in the five-step data science process introduced in the previous chapter (see Figure 3.1).

There are many programming languages and software libraries producing a vast range of powerful and accessible tools for those willing to step away from the graphical user interface and expand their programming skills. Some of the main languages, libraries and integrated development environments are discussed. Access to online information and communities of practice, the development of numerous software libraries, and increased sharing of code online has made the task of programming far easier than it was even ten years ago, and no one who has reached this stage of this book should be daunted by the prospect of programming (although it is not a prerequisite for finishing the book).

Finding tools

This chapter introduces some tools available to data scientists, but it is by no means prescriptive or set in stone. It is more important that information professionals as data scientists are agile and adaptable than that they have any particular expertise in any single technology. Data scientists must be aware of the new tools and programming libraries that regularly emerge, and be willing to experiment with and explore them.

Data scientists should evaluate the suitability of the new tools for specific applications, constantly exploring and learning. This does not have to be an onerous formal activity, organising funding for trips to summer schools and workshops, but rather requires a willingness for independent learning. Sometimes it may be necessary to supplement the independent learning with more formal training, but the many tools available and the iterative nature of applying them to data science challenges means that independent learning is generally a necessity. Unfortunately it increasingly seems as though job advertisements list highly specific technological skill requirements, when what is actually required is the far more difficult to measure ability and willingness to explore new technologies as they emerge.

While the increase in open source software and the number and variety of tools available for data science is of great value to would-be data scientists, the quantity of software available nevertheless creates difficulties when identifying tools and judging their suitability for a particular task. Much of the software that has been made freely available may be quite niche, has little in the way of a user community or documentation, or is no longer supported, all of which can create difficulty in finding the most appropriate tools with a traditional search engine. It is therefore important to use (virtual) communities of practice and some horizon scanning. For example through the question-and-answer services of Stack Exchange:

- Data Science Stack Exchange (https://datascience.stackexchange.com)
- Open Source Stack Exchange (https://opensource.stackexchange.com).

And browsing certain software publications:

- The Journal of Open Source Education (https://jose.theoj.org)
- The Journal of Open Source Software (http://joss.theoj.org).

Every data scientist has their own particular set of tools suitable for their own specific applications, and fitting in with the limitations imposed by such things as cost and ease of use. We should no more expect two data scientists to have the same workflow or set of tools than we would expect two people to have the same set of books on their bookshelves; while there may be some books in common, most shelves of books are unique. The best tool is often the one information professionals are most comfortable with (Boman, 2019).

Software for data science

A variety of software may be used throughout the data science process, and each of them is typically a lot easier to use than learning how to program.

However, depending on the data and type of analysis you want to carry out, it may be necessary to learn to use multiple different tools at different stages of the data science process. This section mentions some of the most useful, focusing on those that are powerful, accessible and, importantly, free.

Data collection

There is a wide variety of data on the web, and a wide variety of tools available for collecting data from it. These may be broadly split into three types: general web tools, data specific tools and service specific tools.

General web tools

As well as the many data files published on the web, the web itself is also data, and there are many tools available for downloading it, the most notable of which are web crawlers and web scrapers.

A web crawler (also known as a spider or robot) is a program that when given one or more seed URLs downloads the HTML, extracts the embedded links, and visits each of the identified links in turn. They have an important role on the web when indexing websites for search engines, and copying sections of the web for archival purposes. There are several free and open source web crawlers available, such as Heritrix (https://github.com/internetarchive/heritrix3) and Nutch (http://nutch.apache.org), and they differ in the way they extract URLs and their crawling strategies (how links are prioritised and how deep a website is crawled). In most instances researchers are not interested in the raw HTML but data contained within it, and for this a web scraper is not only more suitable, but generally far more user-friendly than a web crawler.

A web scraper not only crawls the web, but extracts specific sections of data from it. This is particularly useful where web pages are generated automatically from a database, and similar information is found in the same place on multiple web pages, for example, academic staff pages are often generated automatically, with publications lists found in the same place on each page. There are many web scrapers available, often adopting a subscription or freemium model (where basic services are free but payment is required for more advanced functionality). Portia (https://github.com/scrapinghub/portia) is an open source visual scraper, so no programming knowledge is required. Once it has been installed you simply create a spider, add starting pages, define the crawling strategy and visit some sample pages where you can click on those parts that you want to extract.

GNU Wget (www.gnu.org/software/wget) and curl (https://curl.haxx.se) are programs for downloading content that can be run from the command line. They can be used to download HTML files from the web and other files shared via web protocols. For example, it is possible to download multiple files at once via the command line. There is a recursive retrieval function on GNU Wget which makes it not much more difficult for data to be scraped from multiple pages on a website than a single page.

Data specific tools

There are mainstream tools for downloading specific types of data from the web. For example, even mainstream software such as Microsoft Excel or Google Sheets can be used to import data directly from the web.

Google Sheets includes the functions IMPORTHTML, IMPORTXML, IMPORTDATA and IMPORTFEED. IMPORTHTML is used to import tables or lists from a URL by providing a URL, data type and the index for the section of the page required. This example would import the second table from Wikipedia's medal table of the 2016 summer Olympics:

```
=IMPORTHTML("https://en.wikipedia.org/wiki/2016_Summer_Olympics_
medal_table", "table", 2)
```

IMPORTXML can be used to import XML from the web by providing a URL and an XPath query identifying the relevant elements in an XML document. XPath is returned to in the section 'Data transformation and cleaning', below. This example would search Open Corporates for information companies, and extract their names from the resulting XML results:

```
=IMPORTXML("https://api.opencorporates.com/v0.4/companies/search?q=
information+science&format=xml","//name")
```

Similar queries may be entered in Microsoft Excel, which has a graphical user interface for extracting HTML elements from web pages, and OpenRefine (http://openrefine.org), a data cleaning tool discussed below, can import data directly from the web, a Google Sheet or certain databases.

Service specific tools

The rise in interest in web data has been driven in part by the huge rise in content shared on social media services such as Twitter and Facebook. Twitter in particular has gained a lot of interest because it is open by default and has included an extensive range of APIs from the beginning to encourage adoption and development.

Social media analysis tools vary considerably from those that are free, free to researchers or commercial services. Social media data collection tools is a dynamic area, with new tools and functionality emerging and others disappearing. The focus here is on those that have a useful free element, and have already demonstrated an element of longevity, although all are subject to the whims of their creators and the social media service APIs that they use.

Netlytic (https://netlytic.org) is a cloud-based tool, which uses public APIs to collect data from Twitter, Instagram, YouTube and Facebook. It has three levels of access, from the free tier 1, which allows data sets of up to 2,500 records, to tier 3 (paid for), which allows data sets of up to 100,000 records. It provides simple basic text and analysis and visualisation functionality. SocioViz (http://socioviz.net) is another cloud-based service that collects and visualises Twitter data and networks, albeit on a smaller scale than Netlytic.

Typically more data can be accessed more cheaply when you run the programs yourself. The Statistical Cybermetrics Research Group at the University of Wolverhampton has produced two main social media data collection tools: Webometric Analyst 2.0 and Mozdeh. Webometric Analyst 2.0 (http://lexiurl.wlv.ac.uk) collects and analyses data from many social media services, including YouTube, Twitter and Flickr, and various other online services including search, citation and altmetric services for impact type analysis; Mozdeh (http://mozdeh.wlv.ac.uk) focuses on a more select set of text-based social media services for text and sentiment analysis. Undoubtedly one of the easiest and cheapest ways of accessing Twitter data is to use Twitter Archiving Google Sheet (TAGS; https://tags.hawksey.info), a Google spreadsheet template that allows you to download tweets for different hashtags automatically.

Table 4.1 shows the functionality offered by the tools mentioned above to collect Twitter data for the different packages offered (in June 2019). Data is typically limited to that of the last 7–14 days, and the limited number of

Table 4.1 Comparison of four Twitter data collection tools

Service	Cost (12-month non-profit or academic)	Twitter data
Netlytic Tier 1	free	1,000 most recent tweets
Netlytic Tier 2	by request	1,000 most recent tweets
Netlytic Tier 3	CAD$228	1,000 most recent tweets, can run every 15 mins
SocioViz – anyone	free	100 tweets
SocioViz – associate	€49	5,000 tweets
Mozdeh	free	Twitter API limits, can run every 15 mins
TAGS	free	Twitter API limits, can run every hour

tweets that can be collected generally makes some of the services more suited for collecting data on relevantly quiet hashtags (e.g. #librarylife) rather than extremely popular hashtags (e.g. #brexit). Twitter's API currently allows 180 queries to be sent every 15 minutes, allowing up to 72,000 tweets an hour!

Although social media sites gather the most headlines online, social media is not the only structured data on the web and, as has already been mentioned, Webometric Analyst provides access to some of these other data sources. Information professionals are likely to be particularly interested in its functionality for citation analysis data from Microsoft Academic Graph and altmetric data from Altmetric (www.altmetric.com). Publish or Perish (https://harzing.com/resources/publish-or-perish) is another tool for using online citation services, gathering data from Google Scholar data as well as Microsoft Academic Graph.

Data transformation and cleaning

There are many data cleaning and transformation tools, but here we restrict ourselves to considering two: OpenRefine and Saxon. OpenRefine (http://openrefine.org) is probably the most widely used standalone free tool and the largest proportion of its users are librarians (OpenRefine, 2018). While OpenRefine is extremely powerful when dealing with tables of data, it is less suitable for cleaning and transforming more hierarchical data such as XML. A better way to transform XML from one format to another is to use eXtensible Stylesheet Language Transformations (XSLT) and the command line of Saxon (http://saxon.sourceforge.net).

OpenRefine

OpenRefine is a powerful open source data wrangling tool and particularly useful for information professionals starting on their data science journey as its popularity makes it the topic of numerous online tutorials, and there is a curated web page highlighting some of them (GitHub, 2019).

OpenRefine (originally Google Refine) provides a program for exploring and manipulating tables of data through the browser, although the program and data are stored locally on your desktop. It is designed to facilitate the filtering of data by different facets, and editing multiple cells at a time (hundreds or thousands where possible), for example, removing trailing spaces in cells, standardising capitalisation, or dealing with null values. Here we consider three uses of OpenRefine to help demonstrate its practical use to information professionals: clustering of textual elements, a scatterplot matrix of numerical elements, and joining tables.

Inconsistency in entity names is a common problem when dealing with any large data set, and OpenRefine incorporates several clustering algorithms to help identify differently named entities that may refer to the same one. No organisation is immune from the problem of authority control. For example, the British Library has published CSV files of those contracts worth over £10,000 (British Library, 2020), but despite decades of work in the information profession on authority control, the same organisation often has slightly different names. The Levenshtein distance is one metric to measure the difference between two sequences of characters. Figure 4.1 shows OpenRefine's Levenshtein distance algorithm used to analyse the British Library's 2010 data set. It identifies six possible clusters; some are obvious and may be selected and merged straight away, others may require further exploration.

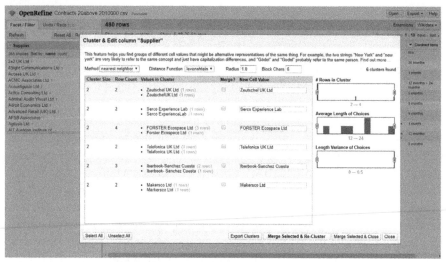

Figure 4.1 *Levenshtein distance used to cluster the 'supplier' to the British Library in OpenRefine*

As well as clustering and editing cell values manually, OpenRefine enables data to be transformed using 'expressions', and has its own General Refine Expression Language (GREL). For example, if you wish to convert some prices from one currency to another, split a data-time field into its requisite parts, or simply inform OpenRefine the values in the table are years, this can be done with a GREL expression.

When exploring a numeric data set, scatterplots are a useful way to explore relationships between different facets, and OpenRefine can create scatterplots for each pair of numerical columns in a data set. Figure 4.2 on the next page shows the scatterplot matrix for the results of the UK's 2014

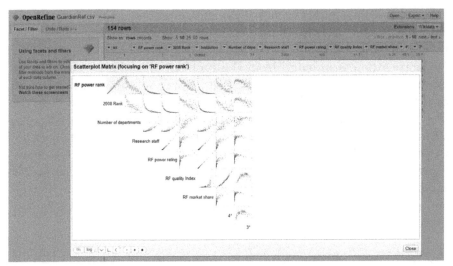

Figure 4.2 *Scatterplot matrix showing the results of the UK's 2014 REF in OpenRefine*

Research Excellence Framework (REF; Guardian Data Blog, 2014). Selecting one of the scatterplots enables it to be explored, clicking and dragging over the graph to select the accompanying records.

New insights from data are particularly likely to emerge when more than one data set is combined, and OpenRefine may be used to reconcile entities with an external data source and to join two tables. The default reconciliation service is with Wikidata (https://www.wikidata.org/wiki/Wikidata:Main_Page), and additional reconciliation services may be added. For example, Conciliator (https://github.com/codeforkjeff/conciliator) is a reconciliation data service that includes Virtual International Authority File and Open Library data. Where more than one data set uses the same unique identifiers, or the same field has been reconciled with the same data service, it is a simple process to then look up values from another.

For example, the UK university research excellence data mentioned above may be combined with other sorts of data about the university, the students or the local area, or even about library fines, which has been collected from each of the institutions and made publicly available (Payne, 2017). If the library fine 'name of institution' column has been reconciled with Wikidata, and Guardian search REF data 'institution' column has been reconciled with Wikidata, then combining data from the two tables is as simple as selecting for the appropriate column **Edit column >> Add column based on this column** and stating which cell to match on, and which cell to add:

```
cell.cross("GuardianREF", "Institution").cells["RF power rating"].value[0]
```

Multiple OpenRefine tables may be reconciled directly by installing the reconciliation service Reconcile-csv (http://okfnlabs.org/reconcile-csv/).

Saxon

To a certain extent, it may be argued that XML has now been superseded by JSON, but with so many applications that either export data in an XML format or have the potential to export data in an XML format, it is worth highlighting one piece of software that can ease its transformation.

First it is necessary to know a little about XML. The document mark-up language XML is designed for sharing hierarchical data in a self-descriptive manner. For example:

```
<example>
 <subject>XML</subject>
 <purpose>To explain what Saxon can do</purpose>
</example>
```

The tags (the terms between the angle brackets) aren't predefined in XML, but are created by the creator of the document. The creator may adhere to some existing standard, or come up with their own set of tags, either way it can be valid XML and the data shared (even if an idiosyncratic selection means the receiver of the data doesn't know what to do with the data).

The XML specification (how you form valid XML) has various other associated specifications. These include XSLT, XML Query (XQuery) and XML Path Language (XPath). XPath enables people to refer to specific elements and attributes in an XML document, and it is used in an XSLT file to refer to the different parts of the document that you want to transform. XQuery is a querying language for XML data.

Saxon (http://saxon.sourceforge.net) is an XSLT and XQuery processor, which can be run from the command line. If you have an XML file that you want to transform, and an XSLT file that describes the nature of the transformation, Saxon can generate the transformed data.

Data analysis

There are too many tools available for data analysis to mention in any detail, so here we restrict ourselves to a discussion of some of the criteria you may use when selecting data analysis software, and some notable examples of each.

Type of analysis

The first question is inevitably: what type of data analysis do you wish to carry out? Data exploration will already have started at the data cleaning stage, and you will already have a good idea about the type of analysis you wish to carry out. While some software can do many types of analysis, certain software is inevitably better suited for some than others. For example, Weka (https://www.cs.waikato.ac.nz/ml/weka) is a workbench of software with many machine learning algorithms for clustering, classifying and regression analysis. If you only want to carry out the occasional linear regression analysis or network analysis, you may be better off with the Excel on your desktop or downloading specialised network software such as Gephi (https://gephi.org).

Cost

For every piece of commercial software there is generally a free alternative available. This may be an open source alternative, with a (potentially) vibrant community of developers swarming over the code and rapidly developing functionality and fixing bugs, or simply a free at point of use piece of software that an individual or research group has made available as a final product. While 'free' is obviously an important consideration when selecting software in times of austerity, 'free' may incorporate additional costs at a later date if you have to develop functionality or there is a lack of documentation.

Table 4.2 provides some examples of free and commercial software that might be used in the data sciences, from qualitative analysis software through to mapping software. Data analysis software can incorporate much complementary functionality and no two pieces of software are likely to be exactly comparable.

Table 4.2 *Commercial and free data analysis software*

Analysis	Commercial	Free
Qualitative data analysis	NVivo	RQDA
Linear regression analysis	Excel	LibreOffice
Data visualisation	Tableau	RAWGraphs
Machine learning	Neural Designer	Weka
Geographic information	ArcGIS	QGIS

Ease of installation

Ease of installation can be as important a factor as cost: there is little point in software being free if it can't be installed. At the easiest end of the spectrum, no installation is necessary; the software exists in the cloud and all you need to do is sign up for an account (e.g. Google Sheets). At the more complicated end of the spectrum dedicated server space may be necessary, especially if it is designed to have multiple users working on data at the same time. Even if software is designed to work on the desktop, it may require additional dependencies or administrator privileges that have been locked by IT services for security purposes. IT services may be more willing to agree to the installation of commercial software with an identifiable organisation taking responsibility than an open source alternative with no one taking responsibility.

It is therefore worthwhile to start by considering what is already available. Most PCs already have a spreadsheet of some sort, and it is remarkable how much data analysis can be achieved in Excel, even without using its incorporated programming language (VBA). But just because something can be achieved in a spreadsheet doesn't mean it is necessarily the quickest or most efficient way of doing it, especially if it is a task that is to be repeated many times.

Ease of use

Software that is already on your desktop is not only easy to install, but is likely to have been used previously, and the difficulty in learning new software should not be underestimated, especially when considering an integrated analytics platform that is designed to help you manage a whole workflow from beginning to end, e.g. the Konstanz Information Miner (KNIME, www.knime.com). Software that focuses on one particular aspect of data analysis is likely to be simpler to understand, so if you are only interested in one particular aspect of data analysis (e.g. cluster analysis) then it is probably easiest to use software that focuses on that.

Size of software community

Every piece of software has developers and users, and the size and permanence of both can have important implications for its long-term support and development. Commercial offerings without a sufficiently large community of users may be unviable and quickly discontinued; open source software without a sufficiently large number of developers may have various bugs; free software designed by a research group may stop development when research funding comes to an end. There are always exceptions to the rule, the lone developer who continues to improve and release a piece of freeware over a long period, but generally a large community of users and developers is necessary for software to be sustainable. It is important for the development of the software and resources helping people use it.

The web provides access to not only a vast array of software, but also many teaching resources for commercial and free data analysis software; if your software is widely used you are more likely to find either solutions to any problems you have, or someone to answer a query online. There are now many high quality software tutorials and MOOCs available online, as well as vast online communities of practice, for example:

- Research Data Management Training (MANTRA; https://mantra.edina.ac.uk/softwarepracticals.html)
- Programming Historian (https://programminghistorian.org)
- data science courses at Coursera (https://www.coursera.org/courses?query=data%20science)
- Data Science on Stack Exchange (https://datascience.stackexchange.com).

Visualisation is often an important part of much of the data analysis software, as well as presenting findings, and special attention is given to that in the next section.

Data visualisation

The tools available for data visualisation are now extremely powerful, enabling the creation of complex and engaging diagrams, but in the same way that data analysis does not necessarily require new software, neither does data visualisation. As Nussbaumer Knaflic (2015) shows in *Storytelling with Data*, striking visualisations can be achieved with the humble spreadsheet and adherence to simple design principles. In this section the focus is on visualisation tools specific to data science, rather than general presentation or graphing tools (e.g. PowerPoint or Excel). These are split into three groups: network graphing tools, mapping tools and text visualisation tools.

Graphing tools

There are many freely available network graphing tools; notable examples include:

- Pajek (http://mrvar.fdv.uni-lj.si/pajek), a well-established network analysis program that is particularly strong on the analytic side, with the Pajek-XL and Pajek-3XL versions enabling the analysis of tens or even hundreds of millions of nodes
- Gephi (https://gephi.org), open source software with more emphasis on visualisation, and suited to smaller graphs (of less than a million nodes);

although the built in analytics are not as extensive as those of Pajek, additional plugins have been built for additional analytics and incorporating different types of data
- VOSviewer (www.vosviewer.com), a tool specifically designed for visualising and analysing bibliographic networks, for example, co-author and citation networks.

Mapping tools
There are now multiple mapping tools available, with choropleth maps (where areas are coloured according to an additional variable) and cartograms (where areas are distorted according to an additional variable) simply generated with a few clicks of a button. Software ranges from large fully integrated commercial products, such as ArcGIS (www.arcgis.com) to relatively simplistic free web-based tools, such as Google's My Maps (https://www.google.com/mymaps) or Google's GeoCharts (https://developers.google.com/chart/interactive/docs/gallery/geochart).

There is much geographic data available online, facilitating the analysis of information by different types of area, for example, national boundaries at Natural Earth (www.naturalearthdata.com), political boundaries at the Open Geography portal of the Office for National Statistics (http://geoportal.statistics.gov.uk) or postal boundaries at GB Postal Area, a dataset within Edinburgh's DataShare (https://datashare.is.ed.ac.uk/handle/10283/2597).

Data scientists who require extensive functionality in a geographic information system, without the associated costs of ArcGIS, can use QGIS (www.qgis.org), an accessible and freely available alternative. QGIS has a large user community, so there is a variety of tutorials available online, and various plugins for analysing geographic data, integrating data from other sources, and displaying the data in different ways. Particularly useful from a visualisation perspective is the cartogram plugin. For large data sets the plugin can be temperamental, but the standalone java program ScapeToad (http://scapetoad.choros.place/) provides an alternative method of generating cartograms.

As with any popular area of discussion, there is a question-and-answer platform at Geographic Information Systems Stack Exchange (https://gis.stackexchange.com).

Text visualisation tools
The visualisation of numbers, networks and maps is in many ways more instinctive than the visualisation of text, although as the Text Visualization Browser (http://textvis.lnu.se) shows, there are many ways text can be visualised. It may be transformed into network graphs, incorporated into

maps or quantified into textual data for traditional graphs, word clouds and morphable word clouds. Here two examples are given, word clouds and a streamgraph.

Word clouds visualise the frequency of terms in a document (or set of documents) by varying the size of the terms according to how frequently they appear. Depending on your point of view they are either a simple, intuitive way to represent the contents of a corpus, or a 'shoddy visualization' and the 'mullets of the Internet' (Harris, 2011). Much of the enmity towards word clouds is driven by their ubiquity and inappropriate use. Too often word clouds are used as a substitute for proper textual analysis, with the overly simplistic splitting of consecutive terms and crude removal of stop words resulting in baffling findings. For example, Harris (2011) highlights how an analysis of Tea Party feelings about Obama found 'like' and 'policy' to be two of the biggest terms, primarily due to the stop word 'don't' being removed. But just because word clouds are often misused, that doesn't mean they can't be a useful form of visualisation. They should just be analysed with more caution than they generally are. Figure 4.3 illustrates a more circumspect use of word clouds than generally appears, showing word clouds of the most popular title words of the 500 most cited library and information science articles in 1974 and 2018 in Web of Science.

Each of the word clouds has been created with the free online tool at www.wordclouds.com. Although Figure 4.3 displays little information about the absolute number of times the terms appear in the titles of journal articles, it nonetheless conveys an overall impression of the changing nature of the

Figure 4.3 *Cloud words of the most common article titles in 1974 and 2018 in Web of Science*

field of library and information science. It is better seen as a method of exploration than a provider of rigorous answers.

Stream graphs may be used to give an overview of changes in the terms used over time and, as for the word clouds, reaction has been polarised (Byron and Wattenberg, 2008). A stream graph is a type of stacked graph, smoothed and flowing around a central axis. While they lack clear quantifiable values, they nonetheless make it possible to demonstrate a broad overview of changes over time. Figure 4.4 shows the rise and fall of various information metric terms during the 21st century. The data has been collected from Web of Science, and is displayed using RAWGraphs (https://rawgraphs.io). It clearly shows the growth and continued dominance of 'bibliometrics' in comparison to other more recent types of metrics (such as altmetrics and webometrics).

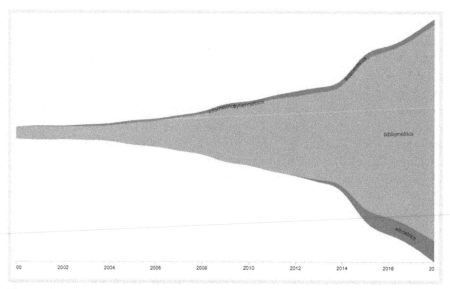

Figure 4.4 *Streamgraph comparing the term 'bibliometrics' and its would-be usurpers (including 'altmetrics' and 'webometrics') on Web of Science, 2000–18*

Some of the best free tools for graphs and charts are the libraries that have been developed for the different programming languages.

Programming for data science

To a certain extent the distinction between software applications for data science and programming for data science is a false one, with diverse types of software being accessible through a graphical user interface (GUI) and programmatically via an API, though some applications (e.g. Microsoft Office applications) have an extensive programming language already built in (e.g.

VBA). Whether you decide to interact one way or another with an application may depend on whether the particular functionality already exists via the GUI or how many times a particular task has to be repeated.

As has already been mentioned, information professionals don't need to be professional programmers to gather and manipulate data, but like the bricoleur, can use 'devious means compared to those of the craftsman' (Lévis-Strauss, 1966, 16–17). In fact bricoleurs are probably more suited to data science than craftsmen, as they are more agile and adaptable than craftsmen who have expertise in a single technology. If you are agnostic about which programming language to use, you are more likely to be able to build on the work of others than if you prefer one over another. As Semeler, Pinto and Rozandos put it (2017, 778): 'A data librarian need not become a programmer, but should be interested in learning about the languages and programming logic of computers. . . . In short, it is the duty of librarians to acquire skills in data processing, to fulfil the tasks of a data scientist.'

Armed with an understanding of just a few basic programming concepts, applicable in most high level programming languages (those understandable to humans), it is a relatively simple process to piece together working code to collect and manipulate data. The way the concepts are actualised and a language's terms and syntax differ, but the web is filled with tutorials and examples to introduce you to the language of your choice (or necessity). The widespread application of programming has even led to developing programming tutorials aimed at particular communities, rather than focusing on particular languages or technologies. For example, The Programming Historian (https://programminghistorian.org) provides novice-friendly peer-reviewed tutorials for those in the humanities with lessons ranging from the principles of linked open data to creating mobile augmented reality experiences, and MANTRA is a free online course for those who use digital data (https://mantra.edina.ac.uk/softwarepracticals.html).

Even if a tutorial, or Google, fails to provide the answer you require, the web provides a vibrant community of programmers to help. The question-and-answer website Stack Overflow (https://stackoverflow.com) claims over 50 million monthly users, many of whom build their reputation as programmers by answering people's queries. If you wish to explore the sorts of questions that are asked in a more methodical manner, Stack Overflow has an API of its own: https://api.stackexchange.com/docs.

Languages

This book is not designed as an introduction to programming; it is an introduction to data science, for which programming is an extremely useful skill. As can be seen from the examples throughout the book, quite a lot can be achieved with relatively little programming knowledge by building on the work of others. All that is required is an understanding of a few basic concepts (variables, functions, loops). These are briefly covered in the Appendix, which gives simple examples for R and Python.

R and Python are only two of the many hundreds of computer languages available. The Hello World Collection (http://helloworldcollection.de) provides a simple 'Hello World' program in 591 languages, while 99 Bottles of Beer (www.99-bottles-of-beer.net) promises 1,500 languages and variations for generating the repetitive lyrics to the song. Unsurprisingly, the majority of these languages are not necessarily of practical use to the average information professional; you may be interested in learning how to program a 1960s super computer or a 1990s graphing calculator, but it's unlikely to have practical applications in your day-to-day work.

Which is the most important programming language depends heavily on what you want to do with it, and which language the community uses. This book uses Python and R: Python because of its versatility and widespread use, and R because of the statistical packages that have been built for it.

Python regularly appears high up on the list of the 'top' or 'most popular' programming languages, with its specific ranking depending heavily on the criteria used. The TIOBE Index of popular programming languages (www.tiobe.com/tiobe-index) ranked it as the third most popular language in June 2019, while IEEE Spectrum ranked it number one for 2018 (https://spectrum.ieee.org/at-work/innovation/the-2018-top-programming-languages). Most important is the fact that it is extremely popular among the data science community, with 52.6% of respondents to the KDnuggets Software Poll using Python in 2017, the highest for any language or tool (Piatetsky, 2017). Python is a high level scripting language, easy to understand and often the first non-visual programming language (as opposed to a blocks programming language such as Scratch) that users are introduced to.

R is less widely adopted, currently only ranked 23rd in the TIOBE Index and 7th on the IEEE Spectrum Index, but it was a close second in the KDnuggets Software Poll, being used by 52.1% of data scientists. R is a statistical language, and has a lot of the more complex data analysis algorithms already implemented.

R and Python are very powerful, extensive languages with active sets of users, and the web is filled with tutorials for them.

Jupyter notebooks

As well as picking the language in which to program, it is also necessary to select and install the software necessary to write and run the code. Although high level code may be written in a simple text editor, such as Windows

Notepad, it nonetheless needs additional software to compile the code into a low level language that the machine can execute. To ease the process of writing, debugging and compiling code there are several integrated development environments available, with the most popular languages having multiple choices with each integrated development environment offering different functionality.

The code in this book has all been created and made available using Jupyter (https://jupyter.org), which can easily be installed using the Anaconda Distribution (https://www.anaconda.com/distribution), which facilitates the installation of additional libraries. Jupyter enables the creation of computational notebooks, which combine simple word-processing functionality with the ability to execute code. Jupyter started as a spin-off of IPython, but now supports multiple languages including R and Python.

Jupyter provides not only a simple environment for writing and documenting code, but one which is easily sharable, and even executable by others over the web. Static versions of notebooks may be viewed with nbviewer (https://nbviewer.jupyter.org), notebooks shared on GitHub are automatically rendered in the browser, and executable versions can be viewed with Binder (https://ovh.mybinder.org).

It is hard to exaggerate the potential of the Jupyter GitHub Binder workflow for data scientists who are able to work in an increasingly open environment. The simplicity with which code may be shared and run by anyone in the world with an internet connection and computer (or smart phone), opens up the data science process to a far wider community. Rather than getting feedback once the final results of a study are written up, it is possible for contributions to be made along the way. It is not necessary to be a programmer to run the code in a notebook or be critical of the steps taken and results achieved. A well-documented notebook merely requires the reader to read the notes and run one cell after another. Those with programming skills can contribute to improving or fixing any problems with the code, or merely learn from another data science example as part of a virtuous learning circle. There has been a paradigm shift in the way we program in data science.

With Jupyter the same integrated development environment supports multiple languages, including Python and R, so it is not necessary to learn the functionality of multiple integrated development environments. The notebooks for this book are available at https://github.com/dpstuart/jupyter. Popular language specific integrated development environments include RStudio (https://rstudio.com) for R and Spyder (www.spyder-ide.org) for Python.

Modules, packages and libraries

The real power of programming rather than proprietary tools is the large amount of external code to build on. The terms module, package and library have different meanings for different languages. In Python a module is a file of functions or classes for reuse, a package is a directory containing a collection of these modules, and a library is often used informally for a collection of core modules. In R, however, packages are functions, data and code in a particular format, and the library is the directory within which it is stored. Rather than getting bogged down with the nuances of the terms, the term library is used throughout this book to refer to stable code that has been made available for download and reuse for others.

For those using the Jupyter notebook installed using the Anaconda Distribution, many of the most popular libraries can be simply installed via Anaconda (https://docs.anaconda.com/anaconda/packages/).

Useful Python libraries

There are Python libraries available on every conceivable subject. In July 2019 the Python Package Index (https://pypi.org), a repository for Python software, listed 185,866 Python projects ranging from extensive frameworks to specialist software for very specific tasks. Any list of the most useful libraries will be as noticeable for what is excluded as what is included. Nonetheless, data scientists should be aware of the six Python libraries used in this book in Chapter 5, 'Clustering and social network analysis', and the principal functionality for which they are likely to be used (although extended functionality of a library is generally far greater than that mentioned here): pandas, Requests, NetworkX, Matplotlib, NumPy and scikit-learn:

- pandas (https://pandas.pydata.org): a library for data manipulation and analysis; data frames are the workhorse for many of the examples in this book, enabling the easy manipulation and updating of tables of data, and pandas provides data frame functionality for Python
- Requests (http://docs.python-requests.org/en/master/user/quickstart): a library for sending and receiving HTTP requests that is easy for people to understand
- NetworkX (https://networkx.github.io): a package for the creation and analysis of complex network graphs; it is not a drawing package for Python, although it has basic functionality, and recommends that graphs are visualised in dedicated software (e.g. Gephi)
- Matplotlib (https://matplotlib.org): a 2D plotting library
- NumPy (www.numpy.org): a library supporting large-scale multidimensional matrices

- scikit-learn (https://scikit-learn.org): a library for machine learning built on the NumPy and Matplotlib libraries mentioned above.

Many other Python libraries are not used in this book, but may be of use at different stages of the data science process. Libraries that can help with the data collection stage include those designed for collecting data from the web and for collecting specific data types or even specific resources:

- Scrapy (https://scrapy.org): a Python library for scraping and crawling the web
- PycURL (http://pycurl.io): a Python library for downloading data from the web
- Flask-Z3950 (https://pythonhosted.org/Flask-Z3950): a library for querying library catalogues
- Crossref API (https://github.com/fabiobatalha/crossrefapi): a library for accessing data from the Crossref service.

There are useful data transformation and cleaning libraries:

- Beautiful Soup (https://www.crummy.com/software/BeautifulSoup): a library for getting data out of mark-up languages (e.g. HTML, XML)
- pyjanitor (https://github.com/ericmjl/pyjanitor): a library for cleaning data.

The data analysis libraries introduced here provide would-be data scientists with several analysis options to explore, but there are various additional libraries available that may offer alternative approaches, different algorithms or simply greater efficiency, for example:

- Natural Language Toolkit (NLTK; www.nltk.org): the leading natural language toolkit for engaging with natural language in Python
- TensorFlow (www.tensorflow.org): a machine learning library originally developed by Google, and for which they have developed a crash course introduction to machine learning (https://developers.google.com/machine-learning/crash-course).

There is an increasing number of additional libraries for easing the data visualisation process:

- seaborn (https://seaborn.pydata.org): builds on Matplotlib and integrates with pandas to provide more extensive statistical visualisation

- Plotly for Python (https://plot.ly/d3-js-for-python-and-pandas-charts): a Python library for creating interactive visualisations, with a version available for R.

Useful R libraries

R is not used in such a wide variety of scenarios as Python and there are fewer libraries overall, although there are still thousands of packages, with many available at each stage of the data science process. Twelve R libraries are used in chapters 6 and 7 of this book: gtrendsR, rtweet, aRxiv, Syuzhet, tm, topicmodels, quanteda, bursts, ggplot2, openxlsx, fable and tsibble.

Three libraries were used for data collection: gtrendsR (https://github.com/PMassicotte/gtrendsR) is designed for downloading data from Google Trends in R and forms the basis of a data forecast; rtweet (https://rtweet.info) is designed for simple interaction with the Twitter API and is used in this book for a sentiment analysis; and the aRxiv library (https://github.com/ropensci/aRxiv) provides a similar simple R interface for accessing data from the arXiv preprint repository and is used in this book for a topic analysis. Libraries for other specific data resources include rcrossref (https://github.com/ropensci/rcrossref) for Crossref data and guardianapi (https://docs.evanodell.com/guardianapi/) for the Guardian newspaper. Chapter 6 uses the openxlsx library (https://github.com/ycphs/openxlsx) for importing data from Excel spreadsheets.

Data cleaning and transformation is primarily achieved in this book using basic string matching functionality and functions incorporated in the data analysis libraries. It uses tsibble (https://github.com/tidyverts/tsibble), a time series data infrastructure package that adheres to 'tidy' data principles. The tidyverse (www.tidyverse.org) is a collection of packages with a shared underlying approach to data structure; among its useful libraries for data cleaning are stringr (https://stringr.tidyverse.org) for cleaning strings and tidyr (https://tidyr.tidyverse.org) for organising and restructuring tabular data.

Chapter 6 uses fable (http://fable.tidyverts.org), a package designed for analysing and displaying time series data used for forecasting. In Chapter 7, Syuzhet (https://github.com/mjockers/syuzhet) is used for the sentiment analysis, quanteda: Quantitative Analysis of Textual Data (https://quanteda.io) for a frequency analysis, bursts (https://cran.r-project.org/web/packages/bursts) for a burst analysis, and topicmodels (https://cran.r-project.org/web/packages/topicmodels) for a topic modelling example that uses text mining package tm (http://tm.r-forge.r-project.org).

Visualisation in chapters 6 and 7 have used embedded functionality incorporated in the data analysis libraries and the widely adopted ggplot2 (https://ggplot2.tidyverse.org). Additional useful visualisation libraries include Plotly (https://plot.ly/r), which is available for Python, and Leaflet for R (https://rstudio.github.io/leaflet), for creating interactive maps.

5

Clustering and social network analysis

By this stage of the book information professionals should have a good idea of what data science is, the steps involved, and some of the myriad of tools now available. In this and the next two chapters we look more closely at specific techniques that may be applied by information professionals. First, in this chapter, we look at clustering and social network analysis, before moving on to look at the statistical methods for forecasting in Chapter 6, and finally text analysis and mining in Chapter 7.

Clustering and social network analysis enable evaluative and relational insights into a set of networked data. This may be the relationship between people and organisations, the similarity between documents, or the centrality of an entity in a network. This chapter discusses some of the main clustering and social network analysis methodologies, their potential application by information professionals, and how they can be simply calculated, primarily using the example of bibliographic data sets. Clustering based on the content of documents is returned to in Chapter 7 – 'Text analysis and mining', in the form of topic modelling.

Network graphs

Modern social network analysis does not have a neat linear history, but rather has emerged from innovations and interactions between the sub-disciplines of social psychology, social anthropology and sociology for an increasingly mathematicised network approach to understanding social networks (Prell, 2012). The whole world, with the exception of a few isolated individuals and tribes, may be thought of as a giant socially networked graph, and as Milgram's famous paper found it is in fact a small world, where there are on average six or fewer social connections between all people on the planet (Milgram, 1967). The validity of the original paper is open to debate (Kleinfeld, 2002), however the internet and the web have given us access to vast quantities of networked data and similar small worlds have been found in e-mail (Dodds, Muhamad and Watts, 2003) and instant messaging (Leskovec and Horvitz, 2008).

At the same time as social network analysis was developing, library and information science researchers were developing methodologies for analysing their own graph: the bibliographic network. Bibliometrics has been defined as 'the application of mathematics and statistical methods to books and other media of communication' (Pritchard, 1969, 349), and journals, articles, researchers and research groups can all be analysed from the perspective of the relationships between them: references, citations, co-authorship or co-words. The development of the Science Citation Index in the 1960s simplified the process by which researchers could access citation data, enabling various evaluative and relational studies to be carried out, and bibliometrics are becoming increasingly widely adopted. Garfield's journal impact factor (JIF), originally designed to identify the core journals in a field based on those that are highly cited (Garfield, 2006), is being used not only to identify core journals but to rank journals and, even more controversially, rank researchers according to where their work is published. The JIF has been joined by a battery of other metrics for quantifying a researcher's output or impact, most noticeably the H-Index (Hirsch, 2005), as well as different approaches to exploring the relationships with co-citation analysis (Small, 1973), bibliographic coupling (Kessler, 1963) and co-authorship analysis (Logan and Shaw, 1987). There has been increased application of social network analysis methodologies within bibliometrics, calculating metrics based on a whole graph rather than just individual parts of it.

The Web of Science continues to be the principal database used for bibliometric analysis (Stuart, 2018), although other bibliographic databases have been adopted in recent years, including Scopus, Google Scholar and Microsoft Academic, and the methodologies are now increasingly being applied to a range of online networks and graphs. Those researching webometrics, defined as the 'study of quantitative aspects of the construction and use of information resources, structures and technologies on the web drawing on bibliographic and informetric approaches' (Björneborn and Ingwersen, 2004, 1217), recognised the similarities between the web as a network of documents and the citation network (Almind and Ingwersen, 1996). More recently the term altmetrics was coined for using the structured nature of data on massive social network sites to establish alternative filters and indicators of research impact (Priem et al., 2010).

It often seems as though social network analysis of the web is all about Twitter, but the web is filled with a host of networks and sub-networks that may be of interest to information professionals. Twitter may indeed provide novel insights into the social networks surrounding a conference hashtag or a library's followers, but Mendeley may offer insights into research networks, GitHub may offer insights into the connections between programming libraries, and linked data offers potential insights into entities scattered across the web. The challenge can be knowing which network to start with.

Graph terminology

Two simple graphs are represented in Figure 5.1. Both comprise nodes (also known as vertices) represented by the dots and edges (Graph A) or arcs (Graph B) between them. Edges are undirected connections whereas arcs are directed connections. For example, Graph A could be a co-authorship network, which by its nature is undirected; if Author A is a co-author with Author B, then Author B must necessarily be a co-author of Author A, it is a fundamental part of what it means to be a co-author. By comparison, Graph B could be a citation which is directed; if Paper F cites Paper G that doesn't mean that Paper G also cites Paper F, in fact before online publishing and versioning of articles (e.g. preprints) it would have been impossible to have such reciprocal citations without deliberate co-ordination between the papers' authors.

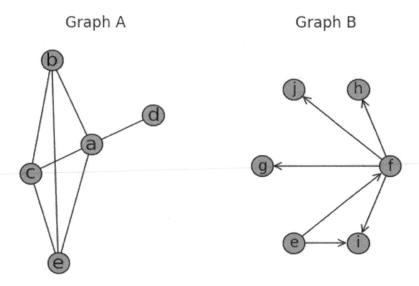

Figure 5.1 *An undirected and a directed graph*

What is actually represented in these graphs is unimportant. The undirected graph could be authors connected by co-authorship, recipes connected by shared ingredients, or cities connected by motorways. A directed graph (or digraph) could be journal articles connected by citations, web pages connected by hyperlinks, or people connected to those they are attracted to. Graphs may be weighted, for example reflecting the number of papers that have been co-authored by two authors. Using directed weightings network graphs may be used to represent data that isn't immediately apparent as network data, for example, sports results may be represented as a graph with the point or goal difference represented as a weighted arc between the teams (nodes), or a Shakespearean play may be represented with the number of words spoken as weighted arcs between the characters (nodes) (Moretti, 2013).

Social network analysis, and to a lesser extent bibliometric ideas, have now gone mainstream with increasingly complex and multifaceted graphs being used to evaluate and segment the market. Social behaviours have been found to cascade through social networks (Christakis and Fowler, 2009); innovation is thought to arise from the interaction of organisations in different sectors (Etzkowitz and Leydesdorff, 2000); and identifying key social mediators can have an important role in engaging with certain communities (Himelboim et al., 2014).

Network matrix
Early social network analysis may have started with the graph first, but today it is necessary to think about how we represent the graph for a computer, and this typically takes the form of a matrix, a two dimensional table representing the network.

Tables of data (whether two dimensions or more) are a fundamental way to represent data in data science; they are typically represented and manipulated within R and Python in data frames and matrices. Whereas a matrix is filled with the same data type, data frames are more general enabling columns of data of different types. Matrices and data frames are built in to R, whereas in Python the pandas library is typically used for data frames, and the NumPy library for matrices.

The same network as Graph A in Figure 5.1 may be represented as a 5 x 5 matrix:

```
matrix([[ 0., 0., 0., 0., 1.],
  [ 0., 0., 1., 1., 1.],
  [ 0., 1., 0., 1., 1.],
  [ 0., 1., 1., 0., 1.],
  [ 1., 1., 1., 1., 0.]])
```

In this case the original graph was created with the NetworkX library in Python and then exported to a NumPy matrix. The numbers may be used to represent the strength between the nodes, and in an undirected graph, the matrix is reflected in the diagonal. The diagonal represents self-links, in some networks this is immaterial (e.g. friending yourself), in others it may be of significant importance (e.g. self-citations).

A table or matrix is not the only way by which a graph can be represented. A sparsely represented graph may be better represented purely by the links that exist between nodes, but it is typically conceptualised as a matrix, with the programming libraries taking responsibility for dealing with the actual data storage and blank spaces.

Boxes 5.1 and 5.2 describe Crossref and how data can be downloaded from Crossref.

Box 5.1 Crossref

Within this chapter social network analysis ideas and concepts are demonstrated using data from Crossref (www.crossref.org), which provides access to over 100 million metadata records to a wide variety of scholarly content types, including articles, books, preprints and data. Importantly these records are available automatically via APIs, and conveniently for those with little data experience, the APIs do not require registration. Crossref requests that users are polite, however, asking that they cache data, monitor response times, and use a User-Agent header so they can be contacted if there is a problem.

Crossref data is explored in this chapter using Python and a Jupyter notebook, available at https://github.com/dpstuart/jupyter/blob/master/Chapter_5_Clustering.ipynb.

It uses four additional imports:

- JSON (https://docs.python.org/3/library/index.html): a module for encoding and decoding JSON, already incorporated in the standard Python library
- Requests (http://docs.python-requests.org/en/master/user/quickstart): a library for sending and receiving HTTP requests that is easy for people to understand
- NetworkX (https://networkx.github.io): a library for analysing graphs and networks; it is not a drawing package for Python, but can be used to display simple graphs and convert data into a format suitable for drawing
- Matplotlib (https://matplotlib.org): a 2D plotting library.

Other libraries have been developed for querying Crossref, in Python (habanero, https://github.com/sckott/habanero) and R (rcrossref, https://github.com/ropensci/rcrossref), although the simplicity of the API and the query used here make them unnecessary.

Box 5.2 Data download from Crossref

The Crossref API is as simple an interface as one could hope for; Crossref has a RESTful API and no registration requirements. For this example, data is downloaded about publications associated with cybermetrics research groups. The search parameters are all encoded in the URI, rather than hidden away in headers, so the results may be viewed in a web browser by visiting the url: https://api.crossref.org/works/?query.affiliation=cybermetrics&rows=100.

The query uses one of the field queries associated with 'works' to retrieve those with the term 'cybermetrics' in the affiliation, and requests the first 100 rows (rather than the default of 20). The query may also be simply sent with Python code:

```
import json, requests
headers={'User-Agent': 'BibExample/0.1 (mailto:info@inforesearch.co.uk)',}
r=requests.get('https://api.crossref.org/works/?query.affiliation=
     cybermetrics&rows=100', headers=headers)
results=json.loads(r.text)
```

results contains the JSON formatted results structured as a Python dictionary (a data type consisting of an unordered collection of key-value pairs), which can then be queried and manipulated.

Visualisation

Visualisation is often an important part of social network analysis, and has been seen as a 'method of exploration' (Moreno, 1978, 96) since the early data of social network analysis. It enables the meaning behind raw numbers to become more immediately apparent. For example, in the simple network graph in Figure 5.2 opposite each of the nodes is linked to four other nodes. If the number of links were taken as a sign of importance, it might be said that all the nodes were equally important. Such a metric would miss an important feature of the network, however; if the central node is taken out the network splits in two with no connections between the two smaller networks. If the nodes and links represent a communication network, there is no way for the information to travel from one side to the other if the central node is removed, whereas any other node may be removed without such a debilitating effect on the whole network.

This is a very simple network diagram with less than a dozen nodes, and there are metrics that would reflect the importance of centrality in the network better than the absolute number of links (see the section 'Node

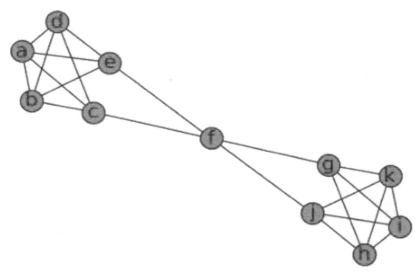

Figure 5.2 *A simple network graph with four links per node*

centrality', below), but the principle remains in far larger networks where a simple single number would fail to reflect the complexity of the network and an individual node's position in it: visualisations are a key part of helping you navigate data, generate hypotheses and understand the relationships between different parts.

Box 5.3 explains how results downloaded from Crossref can be used to build a NetworkX graph.

Box 5.3 Data transformation and cleaning in Crossref

The Python program below takes the **results** downloaded from Crossref to build a NetworkX graph:

```python
import networkx as nx
G= nx.Graph()
for paper in results['message']['items']:
    try:
        authorSet = set()
        for author in paper['author']:
            try:
                name=author['family']+', '+author['given']
                G.add_node(name)
                authorSet.add(name)
```

```
            except:
                print ('Error:no family or given name')
        for x in authorSet:
            for y in authorSet:
                if x!=y:
                    G.add_edge(x,y)
    except:
        print ('Error:no author')
```

The nodes of the graph are based on the authors' names, and three of the authors appear multiple times. These nodes may be contracted:

```
G=nx.contracted_nodes(G, 'Buckley, K.', 'Buckley, Kevan', self_loops=False)
```

The contracting of all three authors reduces the number of connected components to two, one with two nodes, and one with 37 nodes. The largest of the two components is used throughout the rest of this chapter:

```
largest_cc = max(nx.connected_component_subgraphs(G), key=len)
```

NetworkX is not primarily designed for visualising network graphs, and the graphs may be exported in formats suitable for Pajek and other visualisation software. Nonetheless it has some basic visualisation functionality.

```
import matplotlib.pyplot as plt
pos=nx.kamada_kawai_layout(largest_cc)
nx.draw (largest_cc, pos)
nx.draw_networkx_labels(largest_cc, pos, font_size=8)
plt.show(largest_cc)
```

The output of this graph can be seen in Figure 5.3.

Figure 5.3 opposite shows an example network graph, in this case the largest network component of works in Crossref with 'cybermetrics' in the institutional affiliation. The graph revolves around members of the Statistical Cybermetrics Research Group at the University of Wolverhampton. As with all such graphs, it is limited by the quality of the underlying data. Many additional authors are not connected because either the papers or the affiliation are not indexed in the same way.

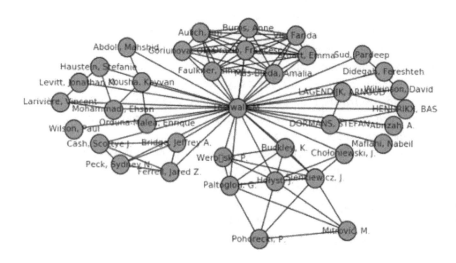

Figure 5.3 *Works in Crossref with the institutional affiliation 'cybermetrics'*

Network analysis

There are broadly three types of network analysis measure: those that measure the properties of individual nodes, those that measure the neighbourhood of a node, and those that measure the structure of the network as a whole (Börner, Sanyal and Vespignani, 2007).

Node centrality

As the name suggests, the centrality of a node in a graph is a measure of how central a node is within the graph, and for many graphs this is taken as synonymous with the importance of the node. For example, an analysis of the co-authorship network of a field may conclude that the most central author is the key author in a field. Centrality has been found to be a useful indicator in a diverse range of areas: the centrality of students in social networks has been found to correlate with a students' academic performance (Ramírez Ortiz, Caballero Hoyos and Ramírez López, 2004); the centrality of authors in co-authorship networks has been found to correlate with citation counts for the authors (Yan and Ding, 2009); and the centrality of streets has been found to correlate with economic activity (Porta et al., 2012).

There are many ways that centrality may be measured, and with different measures identifying different nodes as the most central. Four are used most often: degree centrality, eigenvector centrality, betweenness centrality and closeness centrality:

- *Degree centrality* is based on the number of direct connections a graph has with other nodes in a network. For example, in the simple network graph shown in Figure 5.2, where each node is linked to four other nodes, each node would have a degree centrality of four. Degree centrality ignores the direction of the connections, although there are also the associated indegree and outdegree centrality associated with each node.
- *Eigenvector centrality* is an extension of degree centrality that considers not only the high connectedness of a node, but how highly connected the connected nodes are in turn.
- *Betweenness centrality* recognises nodes as more central when they lie on the shortest route (geodesics) between other nodes. This has been found to capture the most important actors in a network (Prell, 2012).
- *Closeness centrality* recognises a node as having high centrality if it can quickly reach other nodes in a network. Closeness centrality indicates an actor's independence as they do not need to rely on others (Prell, 2012).

Additional centrality measures include: PageRank, a variation on eigenvector centrality used as part of Google's ranking algorithm (Brin and Page, 1998); Katz centrality, which similarly considers the number of routes between nodes; and beta-centrality, which allows the analyst to adjust the importance ascribed to the centrality of others. There are measures of centrality related to cliques and the network as a whole, which are returned to below.

Whether one measure of centrality is preferred to another depends on the subject of the graph. Sometimes the choice of one centrality measure over another is intuitive. If you had a social network graph and you wanted to know who the friendliest person in the graph was, degree centrality would probably make more sense than closeness centrality, as you would not consider someone particularly friendly who just had two friends who happened to be part of two separate social groups. If you were interested in the spread of information in a group, however, you might be more interested in betweenness or closeness centrality.

The way the different centrality measures are calculated makes them suitable for different types of data, and the network may need to be converted before analysis takes place. It is possible simply to convert data values to binary data and directed data to undirected data with graphing software, but the reverse is not possible.

Problems can arise when comparisons are made between graphs of different sizes, and while there are steps that can be taken to normalise for graph size, it is important to be aware of how the normalisation process can itself skew centrality results. For example, degree centrality for a graph may be normalised by dividing degree centrality by the total number of nodes in a graph. So the normalised degree centrality for a node that links six out of ten possible other nodes is 0.6, whereas the normalised degree centrality for a node that links to 10 out of 20 possible other nodes is 0.5. While this process may be suitable for similarly sized graphs, when the graphs are vastly different in size the normalisation can adversely affect the larger graph.

Each of the main measures of centrality can be found on all main network analysis software, as well as being accessible through network analysis libraries. Box 5.4 demonstrates the use of centrality analysis in NetworkX.

Box 5.4 Centrality analysis in NetworkX

NetworkX incorporates many centrality algorithms that may simply be generated about a graph. Below degree centrality statistics are generated for the nodes in the largest connected component of the cybermetrics Crossref graph, sorted by degree centrality as opposed to author name (**key=lambda x: x[1]**) with the largest listed first (**reverse=True**):

```
sorted(nx.degree_centrality(largest_cc).items(), key=lambda x: x[1],
       reverse=True)
```

Calculating alternative centralities is as simple as replacing **degree_centrality** with **betweenness_centrality, closeness_centrality** or **eigenvector_centrality**, as appropriate.

It is important to be aware of any potential differences in the way statistics may be generated. For example, in some software degree centrality is given as an absolute number of connections; in NetworkX degree centrality is normalised according to the number of nodes it could be connected to.

Clustering

Network graphs are rarely homogenous; the links between nodes are often unevenly distributed and entities are clustered together in the same way as they are in the real world. This makes intuitive sense for some networks, such as social networks: those with a large network of friends and acquaintances are likely to be invited to many social events, where they meet some new people but also others whom they already know as friends and acquaintances; within a large network there are small groups of friends who know one another. The preferential attachment of links to those who already have many has been labelled the Matthew effect after the biblical parable of the talents, when the rich get richer and the poor get poorer (Merton, 1968).

The identification of clusters has many applications in developing recommendation systems and market segmentation. It may allow for the identification of invisible colleges, 'a communication network of a subgroup of researchers within a research area' (Crane, 1972, 35), while a recommendation system may use the idea that those who have borrowed or liked similar items in the past will like similar items in the future. This is most famously applied in Amazon recommendations: 'Customers who bought this also bought . . .'

The identification of clusters may be carried out in various ways, depending on the type of data being dealt with. Here we consider first the cliques, n-cliques and k-core of the network graph, before looking at a method clustering entities with multiple attributes using the k-means algorithm.

Cliques, n-cliques and k-core

The idea of a subgroup in a social grouping is often easy for many of us to understand, if not necessarily easy for us to define. We understand that in a classroom of pupils, or a large office of workers, there are smaller groups who work or play together more than they do with those outside the group, but explicitly defining the boundaries of these subgroups can be difficult.

It may be that, as in the co-author network graph of cybermetrics papers in Figure 5.3, there are disconnected components that may be treated as subgraphs, but often it is a far more closely tied network that needs to be split into clusters. Cliques are one way of defining a subgroup, with a clique consisting of a subgraph where every node in the clique has reciprocated ties with every other node in the clique.

Cliques are often considered overly strict. For example, if in a co-authorship network an author was only found to have co-authored with 19 out of 20 people in a clique, then they would not be considered part of the clique. This may be considered especially strict in the case of a directed graph, where it may be that a node is not considered part of a clique despite being linked to by 20 out of 20 other nodes, and linking to only 19 of those nodes in turn. Box 5.5 opposite shows how to explore cliques with NetworkX.

N-cliques allow for greater flexibility, with each pair of nodes connected by a path of n or less. The small world phenomena of many graphs means that n-cliques where n is greater than 3 are meaningless for the purpose of practical analysis.

K-core is another algorithm for identifying clusters where a node is considered part of a k-core if they have a degree centrality of k within that group.

Box 5.5 Cliques in NetworkX

NetworkX includes a number of functions for exploring the cliques of a graph. For example, finding the largest clique number for each node:

nx.node_clique_number(largest_cc)

Or listing the cliques for each node:

nx.cliques_containing_node(largest_cc)

The largest clique for Emma Stuart in Figure 5.4 is 9, this is also the only clique the researcher is part of. Figure 5.4 shows the network graph with the nodes in the clique drawn as white.

```
import matplotlib.pyplot as plt
pos=nx.kamada_kawai_layout(largest_cc)
nx.draw (largest_cc, pos)
nx.draw_networkx_labels(largest_cc, pos, font_size=8)
clique_list=nx.cliques_containing_node(largest_cc, 'Stuart, Emma')[0]
nx.draw_networkx_nodes(G,pos, nodelist=clique_list, node_color='w')
plt.show(largest_cc)
```

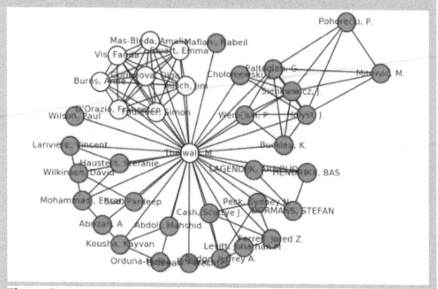

Figure 5.4 *Crossref co-authorship graph, white nodes representing the largest clique for Emma Stuart*

The k-means algorithm

The co-authorship graph provides a relatively simple network, focusing on one type of relationship between two actors, but in many situations the data has multiple attributes that may be used for clustering actors. For example, library books may be (virtually) clustered according to the users who have borrowed them, academic papers according to shared terminology or wider publication information. Although the library community has developed extensive cataloguing and classification systems to help group resources, there are always more resources that haven't been categorised and esoteric collections that require more specialised clusters. The k-means algorithm can help distinguish groupings that have not already been explicitly identified.

The k-means algorithm is an iterative process for sorting actors into a specified number of clusters (k), with each actor being linked to just one cluster. Following a random initialisation for each cluster's centre, the process of assigning actors to a particular cluster and then moving the centroids to the mean of those clusters is repeated.

Although the k-means algorithm is relatively simple to execute, there are some limitations to bear in mind. First, local optima exist, so it is important to try multiple random initialisations and calculate the cost function for each, especially where there is a small number of clusters. Second, there isn't a simple way to determine the appropriate number of clusters, as an additional cluster will produce a better fit for the data until each item is in a cluster of its own. One popular method for determining the appropriate number of clusters is the 'elbow method', where additional clusters stop providing much additional improvement, although unfortunately there's often no clear elbow.

Boxes 5.6 to 5.9 on the following pages show how cluster analysis can be used for data from San Francisco libraries.

Box 5.6 K-means clustering in San Francisco libraries

The k-means algorithm is demonstrated here using data from the City and County of San Francisco on public library usage (https://data.sfgov.org/Culture-and-Recreation/Library-Usage/qzz6-2jup). The data set contains some information about anonymous users' library usage (e.g. number of checkouts and renewals), personal information (e.g. age and contact preferences) and geographic information (e.g. home library).

In this example the k-means algorithm is used to cluster library users. Similar clustering could be used for market segmentation and developing multiple marketing strategies. In this case just two features are used from the data set for ease of illustration: **age_range** and **total_checkouts**.

Multiple additional features could have been incorporated, although multidimensional scaling would then have been necessary to display the results. New knowledge is most likely to be discovered by bringing together data for the first time. Nonetheless the example demonstrates the ease with which the k-means algorithm may be applied and some of the challenges that may be met.

Again the data is explored using Python and a Jupyter notebook; the notebook is available at https://github.com/dpstuart/jupyter/blob/master/Chapter_5_Clustering.ipynb.

It uses five additional library imports:

- pandas (https://pandas.pydata.org): a library for data manipulation and analysis
- NumPy (www.numpy.org): a library for working with a large matrix
- SciPy (https://scipy.org): a library for scientific calculations
- Matplotlib: a 2D plotting library (https://matplotlib.org)
- scikit-learn (https://scikit-learn.org): a library for machine learning that builds on NumPy, SciPy and Matplotlib.

Box 5.7 Data downloading and pre-processing for San Francisco Library users

Data from San Francisco Library users is available online as a CSV file without requiring any authentication, and it can therefore be simply imported into a pandas data frame with a couple of lines of code:

```
import pandas as pd
dataDF = pd.read_csv('https://data.sfgov.org/resource/qzz6-2jup.csv')
```

To use the age range data it needs to be transformed from a string of text into a number, which can be achieved using a dictionary and the pandas **replace()** function:

```
ageDic = {'0 to 9 years' :  5,
          '10 to 19 years' : 15,
          '20 to 24 years' : 22,
          '25 to 34 years' : 30,
          '35 to 44 years' : 40,
          '45 to 54 years' : 50,
          '55 to 59 years' : 57,
          '60 to 64 years' : 62,
```

```
            '65 to 74 years' : 70,
            '75 years and over' : 80}
      dataDF=dataDF.replace({'age_range': ageDic})
```

For the purposes of the example, analysis and visualisation is based on the first 1000 lines of the data frame without missing any missing values:

```
   subsetdf=dataDF.dropna().head(1000)
```

The scales of the two features differ considerably: total checkouts range into the thousands, whereas people's age is much more limited. The relative similarity of all the ages in comparison with the variation in the number of checkouts means that without scaling the number of checkouts dominates the clustering process. This can be seen in Figure 5.5, where age has little impact on the clusters: a 5 year old is grouped with an 80 year old if they have a similar number of checkouts.

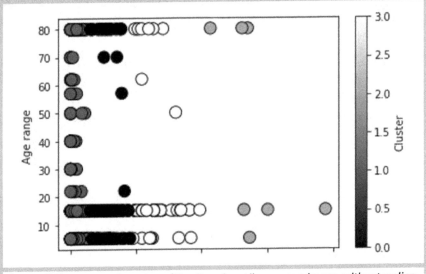

Figure 5.5 *K-means clustering of San Francisco Library users by age without scaling*

Box 5.8 Analysis and visualisation for San Francisco Library users

The scales of the two features may be standardised with the sklearn pre-processing package. The two features are combined in a matrix, scaled appropriately, and the k-means algorithm is applied for a predetermined number of clusters:

```
import numpy as np
from sklearn import preprocessing
from sklearn.cluster import KMeans
f1=subsetdf['total_checkouts'].values
f2=subsetdf['age_range'].values
X=np.matrix(tuple(zip(f1,f2)))
X=preprocessing.MinMaxScaler().fit_transform(X)
kmeans = KMeans(n_clusters=4).fit(X)
```

The results of the k-means algorithm are then stored in a new column in the data frame, which can be used for colouring the clusters. Figure 5.6 shows the scaling of the features with clusters varying according to age and the number of checkouts.

```
subsetdf=subsetdf.assign(Cluster=kmeans.labels_)
subsetdf.plot.scatter(x='total_checkouts', y='age_range', c='cluster',
                      s=128, colormap='gray', edgecolor='black')
plt.ylabel('Age range')
plt.show()
```

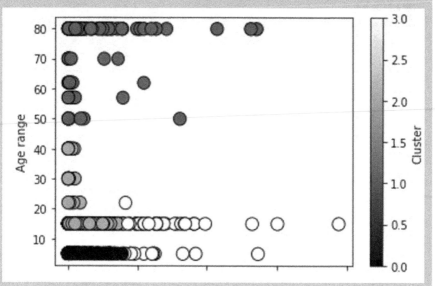

Figure 5.6 *K-means cluster of San Francisco Library users by age with scaling*

Box 5.9 The Elbow Method for San Francisco Library users

In the above analysis the number of clusters was predetermined as 4. The appropriateness of this can be seen when comparing the distortions (the sum of the squared distance between each observation and the centroid of the cluster) for different values of k. While there is a notable drop in the amount of distortion when moving from three clusters to four, there is a far smaller drop beyond this point (see Figure 5.7):

```
from scipy.spatial.distance import cdist
import matplotlib.pyplot as plt

distortions = []
for k in range(1,10):
    kmeanModel = KMeans(n_clusters=k).fit(X)
    distortions.append(sum(np.min(cdist(X,
                        kmeanModel.cluster_centers_,
                        'euclidean'), axis=1)) / X.shape[0])

plt.plot(range(1,10), distortions, 'bx-')
plt.xlabel('k')
plt.ylabel('Distortion')
plt.show()
```

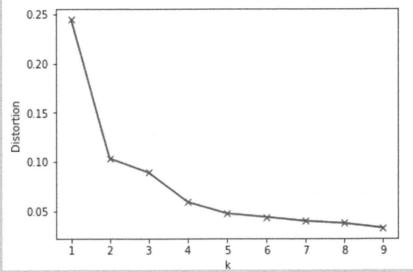

Figure 5.7 *Distortion calculated for San Francisco Library users with different numbers of clusters*

It is important to note that chunks of text, or lists of items (e.g. books borrowed by a library user), may be reduced to features for the k-means algorithm, for example, noting the number of times particular words appear in a section of text. Category data may either be converted to binary values, or use the similar k-mode algorithm.

Graph metrics

As well as metrics that measure properties of nodes and clusters, there are also metrics for measuring properties of a graph as a whole in social network analysis.

The simplest of these graph metrics is density, which may be thought of as reflecting the cohesiveness of the graph. It is the total number of connections in a graph divided by the number of possible connections. For example, in an undirected graph of five nodes, there are ten possible connections: each of the nodes (n = 5) may be connected to each of the other nodes (n−1 = 4) (see Figure 5.8, Graph A), with the number of possible connections divided by 2 as it is undirected ((5 x 4)/2 = 10). If only five of the possible connections actually exist within a graph then the density is 5/10 or a half.

An example of this is where it may be of interest in an academic library to compare the co-authorship network of different departments within an institution: which are the most densely connected departments? Is the

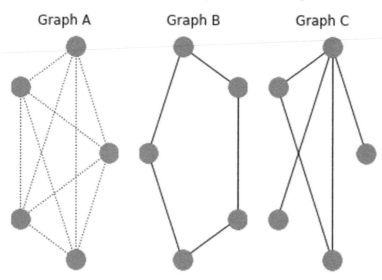

Figure 5.8 *Variations on a five node undirected graph*

underlying cohesiveness of a department reflected in other departmental metrics such as research assessment or student achievement?

As with all metrics, there are inevitable limitations with density. As with degree centrality, discussed above, the size of the graph can affect the density of the graph, and it would be unreasonable to compare graphs of significantly different sizes. We may compare the density of the friendship connections in two classrooms of children, but it would be meaningless to compare the density of friendship in a classroom with that of friendship in a country; the friendship graph of a country would inevitably be more sparse than that of a classroom.

Density alone gives little indication of the distribution of connections in a graph. For example, in Figure 5.8, Graph C has the same density as Graph B, but the distribution of the two graphs is very different. Whereas in Graph B the connections are evenly distributed, in Graph C one node has four times as many connections as two nodes, and twice as many as the other remaining nodes. There is another metric to alert you to reliance of a network's density on a small number of actors: degree centralisation. This and other graph metrics, such as graph diameter (the longest geodesic or shortest path between two nodes) in a network or average path length (the average geodesic length), can typically be quickly and easily calculated with network software or libraries.

6

Predictions and forecasts

Data science is particularly valued for its ability to help predict the future. The desire to predict the future is not new, but while the art of forecasting may have come a long way from divination by chicken bones, it has not necessarily come as far as we might always presume.

The chapter is split into four main parts, narrowing down from predictions in the broadest sense to the practical application for library and information professionals, before looking more closely at statistical methodologies. First it considers the subject of making predictions and forecasts more widely, the importance of recognising the limitations of applying statistical methods to well-defined data sets, and some of the alternative approaches to forecasting. This is followed by an overview of some of the tools and resources that have been used for making predictions with data and the potential application of such methods for library and information professionals. The chapter finishes by looking at the practical application of some specific statistical methodologies: regression analysis and exponential smoothing.

Predictions and forecasts beyond data science

Today's media is filled with an endless stream of forecasts and predictions about what we can expect the future to hold. Alongside our increasingly long-range weather forecasts, our media is saturated with long-term forecasts: central banks make forecasts about inflation and economic growth; health organisations predict the rise or fall of longevity, populations, and the spread of various communicable diseases; and scientists forecast temperature rises and predict the impact of climate change. At the same time there is always an endless stream of pundits ready to predict the doom or utopia just over the horizon for a company, political party or country, based on the various business or political decisions it currently faces. Invariably many of the predictions will be wrong, this is partly the result of conflating forecast and prediction, but mostly because of the complexity of the world.

The terms prediction and forecast are often used interchangeably with reference to anticipated future events, but it can be useful to distinguish the two words by looking at the emphasis they place on existing data. Whereas forecasts are typically more grounded in existing data, predictions may include instances where visions of the future rely on more tangential information. A new technology or innovation has little relevant data on which to base forecasts, and the impact and knock-on effects of the technology may be impossible to predict, as is often seen with disruptive technologies.

Understanding the impact of new technology is not a new problem. In 1932 H. G. Wells lamented that 'though we have thousands and thousands of professors and hundreds of thousands of students of history working on the records of the past, there is not a single person anywhere who makes a whole-time job of estimating the future consequences of new inventions and new devices. There is not a single Professor of Foresight in the world' (Wells, 1932). Today even high street stores have futurologists to help them prepare for tomorrow's retail environment (Heathman, 2018), but such predictions are far from simple as technologies evolve and meet the forces of the market.

The world is a complex and sometimes chaotic system, and there are inevitably unintended consequences and knock-on effects that cascade through it as different components interact with one another. When Tim Berners-Lee proposed a document-sharing system for CERN in the 1980s it seems highly unlikely that he had internet data, streaming box sets and the death of the high street at the back of his mind. When the first iPhone was launched in 2007 there were few smartphone examples for forecasting future sales or even to suggest which functionality would be important to users; in today's world driven by access to millions of apps, it is difficult to imagine the emphasis on phone calls, voicemail and streaming music at the iPhone's launch (Newport, 2019).

While we now have access to great swathes of information, it is necessarily only a limited and rough approximation of the real world. Big data moves us towards a world where $n = all$, but it never quite reaches that point. Adjustments still need to be made to accommodate sampling errors and the difference between how people present themselves in public and what they really think. The problem is we do not always know by how much to adjust, and in the end we may overcompensate. Although the future may promise increasing quantities of interconnected data, there will never be a perfect representation: there are physical limits to the measurement of the world (Heisenberg's uncertainty principle), while the act of observation itself inevitably impacts the system. There will always be black swans, events outside the system that cannot be predicted and overturn the system, and positive feedback, where small disturbances become amplified within the system.

In response to the inevitable unpredictability and uncertainty inherent in all predictions there are many approaches that take more wide ranging tactics to predicting and adapting to the future. Technology foresight, for example, is a 'systematic, participatory, future intelligence gathering and medium-to-long-term vision-building process aimed at present-day decisions and mobilising joint actions' (Miles et al., 2008). The idea is not to predict a single outcome, but rather gather data by applying a range of methods to suggest a variety of possible futures. This includes everything from heavily evidence-based approaches such as literature reviews and bibliometric analysis through to more creative approaches such as science fiction writing or simulation gaming. It may be based on the thoughts of a panel of experts or wider citizens. In a similar vein, scenario planning imagines possible futures and identifies ways of adjusting to meet the challenges of these futures.

Predictions in a world of (limited) data

While acknowledging the limitations of making forecasts on any particular set of data, even with big data, it is nonetheless necessary to recognise that in most situations this is the only option. For example, there are a variety of ways the future number of books issued by a library could be predicted: library users could be surveyed about expected future habits, futurists could predict the effect of new technologies likely to affect people's free time, or social media could be mined for indicators of changes in reading habits. In reality, however, most people base their forecasts solely on the past number of issues rather than coupling it with various other methodologies.

Such data forecasting sits somewhere between divination by chicken bones and fully fledged technology foresight, and while a plethora of data and tools emerge, it is important always to keep in mind the associated limitations and not to over-interpret the data. There are always black swans, unintended consequences in a complex system, and limitations in the statistical methods themselves. As the often repeated statistics mantra states: correlation does not imply causation. This could be clearly seen with Google Correlate, which unfortunately shut down at the end of 2019.

Google Correlate was a powerful tool for exploring correlations between search terms or between search terms and real world trends. Google receives billions of searches each day from all around the world, and Google Correlate enabled users to explore which terms rise and fall together or, alternatively, which terms correlate with an uploaded time series data. The terms did not have to correlate exactly, but could be time-shifted so that one precedes the other. If you uploaded data about house prices or unemployment rates you could find the search terms that correlate with those trends, potentially providing early indicators of real world changes (Stephens-Davidowitz, 2018). The most famous example of the identification of real world changes from online searches was for the early prediction of flu outbreaks based on searches for associated symptoms (Ginsberg et al., 2009). However, early optimism became more muted as the subsequent predictions of Google Flu Trends differed considerably from the reality as reported by the Centers for Disease Control and Prevention. This has been attributed not only to the panics about flu in the media, but big data hubris (the assumption that big data is a substitute rather than a supplement to traditional analysis) and algorithm dynamics (changes to the underlying Google algorithm affecting the data that is collected) (Lazer et al., 2014).

That there is a disconnect between correlation and causation is quickly apparent when searching Google Correlate for specific terms. For example 'library cuts' in the UK was found to be highly correlated with 'whips and chains excite me'. Although it's possible that austerity driven cuts to library budgets led to a rise in sadomasochistic proclivities in the UK, a more likely explanation is the fact that both were isolated spikes that happened to occur at the same time: one occurred because of the coalition's government austerity agenda, the other because the song 'S&M' was released by Rhianna around the same time. Similarly, an occasional note in the *New England Journal of Medicine* has noted the correlation between the number of Nobel Prize laureates and the consumption of chocolate (Messerli, 2012). We have more data than ever before, and there may be new and unexpected correlations, but if we fail to differentiate the signal from the noise we may be doing little more than trying divination with digital chicken bones. Those who said 'correlation supersedes causation' are calming down (Harkness, 2016, 245), although a more circumspect approach to the current trove of data can undoubtedly glean a lot of new insights.

Like weather forecasts, data-based forecasts are best when there is a clearly defined and relatively stable system, a wealth of historical data, and you are not trying to look too far ahead. For example, the travel comparison site Kayak (www.kayak.co.uk) has incorporated price prediction functionality into its website, so that if you search for a flight the site provides a prediction as to whether the cost of the flight is likely to go up or down. Typically, in the short term, the air transport system may be considered to be mostly stable. Weekly and seasonal fluctuations are fairly predictable, and even major international events in one particular place (e.g. Olympic Games and World Cups) are not without precedence. There is always the possibility of major unexpected disruptions that may overturn previous patterns – terrorist activities, erupting volcanoes or unexpected declarations of war between states – but these are thankfully relatively rare occurrences and don't impact the average flight. More gradual longer-term trends, for example changes in attitudes to travelling caused by climate change, are unlikely to have a significant impact on prices in the short term. A future government may add significant additional taxes onto the cost of flights, but this is unlikely to be a surprise tax in the next week, rather it is one that either lies beyond the range of the prediction or has already been signalled.

Unfortunately most predictions are not simple: there is rarely such a wealth of historical data available, we want to make predictions beyond a few days or weeks, and various unexpected events can affect an outcome. No one would have predicted that a woman writing a children's book in an Edinburgh café would have an impact on the trade of owls in Indonesian bird markets a decade later, and yet the correlation with the success of the Harry Potter books can be seen and causation is presumed (if nonetheless difficult to prove) (Nijman and Nekaris, 2017). The world is filled with unexpected connections, and unfortunately all too often the invisible hand of the market will continue to be invisible despite our best efforts.

The vast quantities of data now available from the web and the internet of things offer a host of new possibilities for predicting the future and challenging our narratives about the past. For example, while there may be a tendency to associate every new children's magical fantasy film or novel with Harry Potter, data from Google Books Ngram Viewer (https://books.google.com/ngrams/graph?content=wizard) suggests that the upturn in wizard books preceded the publication of the first Harry Potter book in 1997, and it was a wave it rode rather than one it created.

Predicting and forecasting for information professionals

Library and information professionals are as interested in forecasting the future as any other professional, if not more so. The provision of high quality information services relies on an understanding of the changing demographics of users, changing information habits and technological trends. Unsurprisingly, therefore, several groups have been established to try to understand the future of libraries. These range from the national American Library Association's Center for the Future of Libraries (www.ala.org/tools/future) to the local Chicago-area Library Forecasting Interest Group (https://www.libraryforecasting.com), and they generally focus on potential developments rather than specific hard data, for example, highlighting the emerging blockchain trend rather than trying to quantify its future use.

Making predictions in the information sector is notoriously difficult, with many traditional formats stubbornly refusing to die quietly. For example, the bookless library has been more heralded than realised, and the e-book has a complex relationship with the physical version and has not simply gradually replaced it. In fact the declared success or failure of e-books depends heavily on the particular set of publisher statistics used: whether restricting ourselves to the e-book sales of traditional publishers, or whether we include self-publishing and e-book subscriptions.

In this chapter the focus is more on hard data, extrapolating from existing data sets to forecast future situations. This has many applications in the library and information sector, from predicting growing subject areas, estimating the half-life of books, to even predicting the success of a library's wider institution. This prediction may be based on internal data, sometimes external data, and sometimes a collaboration of the two. While there may be a lot of data in libraries collectively, there is not necessarily a lot of the particular data required in any single individual library.

As with any prediction or forecast, there are inevitably noise, false positives, false negatives and feedback loops for information professionals: changes in library management systems may cause changes in the way statistics are calculated; subject areas predicated to grow may shrink; subject areas predicted not to grow may do so exponentially; while predictions of disaster may help prevent the disaster.

Understanding that you are dealing in probabilities rather than absolutes is an important part of any prediction or forecast. In the same way that weather forecasters increasingly do not say it will or won't rain, but rather forecast the chance of rain, so we should consider the probability of any particular outcome, and the consequences of being wrong. We should not ask ourselves 'Will this book be a blockbuster hit?' but rather 'What are the chances of this book being a blockbuster?', 'What are the consequences of not spotting it early', and based on that, 'What are we willing to invest?' Generally the chance of any particular book being a blockbuster is fairly low, and the consequences of not recognising an upcoming blockbuster equally fairly low for a library (patrons may have to wait a week or two longer). By way of comparison, if the potential consequences of not having a medical matter checked could be that someone dies, even if there is an equally low probability of this occurring as that a new book could be an upcoming blockbuster, it is worth asking a doctor to investigate it.

Being forced to consider the probability of our decisions having any particular outcome allows us to judge our predictions more accurately, ensuring we don't overstate the value of any single prediction. We are often dealing with a chaotic system, and it is important to recognise that no predictions can be expected to be accurate all the time.

Statistical methodologies

Many statistical approaches can be taken to exploring data, and with a large enough sample of data it is generally possible to cherry pick results to support weak arguments. As the often quoted (and widely attributed) phrase has it:

there are also 'lies, damned lies and statistics'. Even the most incompetent private company taking over the running of a public library service will be able to find something in their statistics to crow about, even if overall issues continue to decline: issues for a niche demographic or type of loan may be up, regular seasonal variation may be attributed to innovative policies, or a slowing in the rate of decline may be heralded as a sign of recovery. Libraries should be wary, however, of cherry picking findings for the purpose of public relations. Libraries are often among the most trustworthy sources of information (CILIP, 2018; PEW, 2017), and that trust should not be put in jeopardy for the sake of short-term promotion.

Here we focus on just two statistical techniques: regression analysis and exponential smoothing. In regression analysis the best fit exponential function is calculated for an existing data set, which allows predictions to be made to other data points. For example, a university may wish to identify as early as possible those students most likely to fail a module, and use library usage data as an early indicator. If, in previous years, low library usage has typically been followed by failing a course, then those who have similar usage behaviour may be helped with early intervention. Exponential smoothing is a statistical technique for forecasting the future based on past behaviour, for example, predicting the number of issues by a library if current trends continue.

Regression analysis

Regression analysis estimates the relationship between variables, which are typically labelled dependent (the outcome that is being studied) and independent (the inputs that cause the variation). Once you have modelled the relationship between the independent and dependent variables, you can predict the value of a dependent variable where you only have information about the independent variables. For example, a prediction may be made about a house price (dependent variable) based on the size of the house (independent variable). Alternatively, the number of Twitter followers an account has may be based on the number of updates it has posted, length of time on Twitter, and the number of accounts it is following. Regression analysis predicts a value rather than a specific categorisation, which is the task of classification, although in some instances the regression analysis may form the basis of the classification, for example in the case of logistic regression.

There are many different regression analysis techniques, and here we consider just two: simple linear regression analysis and multiple regression analysis. Linear regression analysis models the relationship between dependent variables and independent variables with a straight line. Simple linear regression analysis typically refers to the use of one independent variable, multiple regression analysis refers to the use of two or more independent variables.

The addition of multiple independent variables can introduce the problem of overfitting. Whereas 90% of the behaviour of variation may be explained by one variable, increasing the number of independent variables may provide a better fitting model, but not necessarily beyond the training data. Independent variables should be independent of one another; multicollinearity refers to independent variables related to one another.

With simple linear regression analysis the statistical package will return an estimated regression equation of the form:

$$\hat{y} = b_0 + b_1 x$$

In multiple regression analysis the statistical package will return a model of the form:

$$\hat{y} = b_0 + b_1 x_1 + b_2 x_2 + b_3 x_3 \ldots b_p x_p$$

In each case $\hat{y}$ (or 'Y hat') refers to the predicted value of the dependent variable, b_0 is the intercept, and b_1 to b_p are the coefficients associated with each of the independent variables, where p is the number of independent variables. Each coefficient relates to the change in y when all other variables remain the same. The values of the coefficients are calculated to minimise the difference between the predicted and actual results.

It only makes sense to base a prediction of the dependent variable on the independent variable if there is a correlation between the two. The correlation between the two variables may be calculated, typically using Pearson's correlation coefficient for continuous data and Spearman's rank correlation coefficient for ranked data. Pearson's and Spearman's correlation coefficients range from $+1$ to -1, with $+1$ being a perfect linear correlation and -1 being a perfectly negative linear correlation. Zero means there is no correlation. Most correlation coefficients fall somewhere in between, and the interpretation of the different coefficient values varies considerably between fields. For example, a correlation of 0.3 may be described as 'weak', 'moderate' or 'fair' (Akoglu, 2018). It is important to distinguish between the strength and significance of a correlation: whereas the correlation coefficient provides an indicator of the strength of the correlation, it is necessary to calculate a p-value to be able to state whether the correlation that is found (whether poor, moderate or strong) is statistically significant. Strength and significance are connected, but they are not the same thing: two weakly correlated variables would require more instances (degrees of freedom) for the significance of the relationship to be demonstrated and the critical value achieved, but however unlikely it is that you would gain the findings by chance, it doesn't increase the strength of the correlation. It is important to remember that however strong and significant the correlation is, it says nothing about causation.

The example explored in Box 6.1, Figure 6.1, Table 6.1 and Box 6.2 on the following pages considers the relationship between the number of followers a Twitter account has (the dependent variable) and various other information associated with the account (the independent variables) using R. Box 6.1 explains how a linear regression analysis can be made of Twitter data, Box 6.2 explains how a multiple regression analysis can be made of Twitter data.

Box 6.1 A linear regression analysis of Twitter data

Social media is an increasingly important part of many libraries and their wider institutions, but gauging the impact of a social media account can be difficult. Should a library with 1000 followers on Twitter be celebrating or lamenting? In this example we explore the relationship between the number of followers a Russell University Twitter account has (the dependent variable) and four independent variables: the length of time the account has been active, the number of tweets sent from it, the number of accounts followed by the account holder, and the number of students at the institution. Each of these variables may be expected to have had an impact on a university's number of followers.

The data for this example has been collated and stored in an Excel spreadsheet in the GitHub directory that accompanies this book (https://github.com/dpstuart/jupyter). The spreadsheet is imported into a data frame using the openxlsx library (https://github.com/ycphs/openxlsx).

```
library ('openxlsx')
TwitterData <- read.xlsx('https://raw.githubusercontent.com/dpstuart/
            jupyter/master/RusselGroupTwitter.xlsx', startRow=2)
```

The correlation between any two variables may be simply calculated with the inbuilt correlation function: **cor()**. By default this is a Pearson correlation (for continuous variables), but an additional argument may be added for calculating Kendall's or Spearman's rank correlation:

```
cor(TwitterData[['Tweets']], TwitterData[['Followers']])
```

As can be seen from Table 6.1 on the next page, none of the analysed independent variables have a positive impact on the number of followers. Plotting the data highlights Oxford and Cambridge as outliers, with far more followers than might be expected according to their Twitter activity or number of students. This is unsurprising, undoubtedly attributable to their high international prestige. Another data frame can be created, dropping the Oxford and Cambridge rows from the table:

```
withoutOxCam <- TwitterData[-c(3,17),]
cor(withoutOxCam[['Tweets']], withoutOxCam[['Followers']])
```

Table 6.1 The Pearson correlation coefficient between the number of followers a Russell Group University Twitter account has and four independent variables

	Pearson correlation coefficient for all Russell	Pearson correlation coefficient for all Russell
'Joined'	−0.113	−0.367
'Following'	−0.018	0.244
'Tweets'	−0.075	0.354
'Students'	−0.140	0.224

There is now a greater correlation between each of the independent variables and the dependent variables. There is a negative correlation for the date joined, because of the way dates are stored in an Excel spreadsheet: a date is the number of days since 1 January 1900, so those that have been on Twitter the longest have the smallest number for 'joined'. That there is only a weak correlation for any of the factors may be expected, as there are multiple different ways of using Twitter and reasons for people to follow different accounts. As none of the correlations are statistically significant one would usually stop at this stage rather than continue to develop a regression equation.

The inbuilt linear model function (**lm()**) returns a linear model for a particular formula with the intercept and coefficient. The **summary()** function returns information about residuals, distributions and p-values:

```
model<-lm(withoutOxCam[['Followers']]~withoutOxCam[['Following']])
summary(model)
```

Scatterplots for the four graphs can be simply generated for each of the independent variables and the dependent variable using the **plot()** function to create the scatterplot and the **abline()** function to put the linear model over the top. For example, for 'Followers' and 'Following':

```
plot(withoutOxCam[['Following']], withoutOxCam[['Followers']])
abline(model, col=2, lwd=3)
```

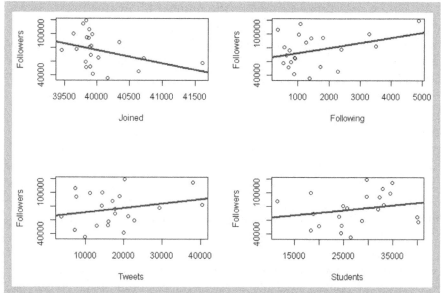

Figure 6.1 *Scatter graphs for four independent variables of a Russell University Twitter account and the number of followers of the account, with linear model lines*

Box 6.2 A multiple regression analysis of Twitter data

As is to be expected, multiple factors contribute to the number of followers an account receives on Twitter, and multiple regression analysis enables a better fit for the available data. Multiple regression analysis uses the same lm() function used above, although with more independent variables:

```
model<-lm(withoutOxCam[['Followers']]~withoutOxCam[['daysJoined']]
    +withoutOxCam[['Following']]+withoutOxCam[['Tweets']]
    +withoutOxCam[['Students']])
```

This generates the coefficients for the following equation:

Followers = (20.49 x days joined) + (6.610 x following)
+ (0.002553 x tweets) + (1.161 x students) – 41,124

The equation does not state how to increase the number of followers, but it may provide some indicators of the types of behaviour rewarded (having a long established account and following other accounts), and it enables an institution to benchmark itself against similar institutions.

If you are only trying to predict the number of Twitter followers you should expect to have, then the form of rough and ready analysis in the example above is enough, but if you are trying to predict more important factors it is important to take a more robust approach to testing your predictions. See the section 'Testing your forecasts' below.

Exponential smoothing

Whereas regression analysis is useful for making predictions based on similar events, exponential smoothing makes predictions of future events based on past events. For example, predicting the number of library loans for a new library can use a regression analysis based on data from other similar institutions (e.g. population demographics, book budget); predicting the number of future loans for an existing library can use exponential smoothing based on the past number of issues.

At its most simple, a prediction may take the average of previous events. For example, if you want to predict the number of visitors to the British Library before they are publicly available, or have even been captured, you can take the data from previous years available from the Association of Leading Visitor Attractions (www.alva.org.uk) and average it. Indeed, if we compare the predicted visitors for 2018 based on the average of the previous years' data that is available, the results are fairly close: 2018 predicted visitors – 1,403,799; 2018 actual visitors – 1,437,839. The number of visitors in some years was much lower (1,113,114 visitors in 2005) and in some years was much higher (1,627,599 visitors in 2014), but the average is fairly close, with the actual value just 2.4% higher than the number predicted for any year. An even closer prediction would have been to take the previous year's number of visitors: 1,426,433 visitors in 2017. The actual value would have been just 0.8% higher.

Predictions reliant on a single figure are more liable to influence by a single outlier: if one year's visitor numbers rapidly increased because of a temporary exhibition which has since closed, it would be foolish to base a future prediction solely on those numbers. Ideally you want to balance the greater importance of recent data points with the overall long-term trend. This is what exponential smoothing tries to achieve.

Exponential smoothing produces 'weighted averages of past observations, with the weights decaying exponentially as the observation gets older' (Hyndman and Athanasopoulos, 2019, 171). When considering visitors to the British Library in the example above, this means that the 2017 data is weighted much more heavily than the 2005 data. There are multiple variations of exponential smoothing, and whole books have been written on the topic. Here we limited ourselves to a broad overview of three types: simple (or single), double and triple.

Single exponential smoothing is designed for use where there is no underlying trend or seasonal pattern. It has a single smoothing parameter (α), which can be set between 0 and 1 depending on the weight you wish to apply to the most recent observation. The higher the number the greater weight that is applied to recent observations. With no discernible overall trend to the British Library visitor data, this would be the most appropriate type of exponential smoothing. Box 6.3 shows how exponential smoothing can be used to predict future visitors to the British Library using the fable package for R.

Box 6.3 Forecasting visitors to the British Library

In this example simple exponential smoothing is used to predict future visitors to the British Library using the fable package for R (http://fable.tidyverts.org), which adheres to the previously mentioned tidyverse structure. It uses the openxlsx library for opening an XLSX file, and tsibble (https://github.com/tidyverts/tsibble) to structure the data in a tidy temporal data frame:

```
library ('openxlsx')
library ('tsibble')
library ('fable')
BLdata <- read.xlsx('https://raw.githubusercontent.com/dpstuart/
    jupyter/master/BritishLibraryVisitors.xlsx')
BLts<-as_tsibble(BLdata, index=Year)
```

The ETS() function returns an exponential smoothing state space model that can be used for forecasting. It can include information about the type of model and whether to include a trend or seasonal variation, although it will choose the model automatically if specific requirements are not stipulated: https://fable.tidyverts.org/reference/ETS.html:

```
fit <- model(BLts, ETS(Visitors))
```

The report() function provides details on the model, its type and parameters:

```
report(fit)
```

In this case the model constructed has been created automatically with an additive error term, no trend and no seasonal variation, and a smoothing parameter of 0.977 (to 3 d.p.). These parameters could have all been stated explicitly:

```
fit <- model(BLts, ETS(Visitors ~ error('A') + trend('N', alpha=0.977)
    + season('N')))
```

The model may then be used to forecast future values:

```
forecast(fit)
```

With no trend and a high alpha, the predicted value is close to the last value: 1,427,343 predicted for 2019 in comparison with the 1,437,839 visitors in 2018.

Double exponential smoothing extends simple exponential smoothing to include a trend, which may be either additive or multiplicative, enabling either linear or exponential growth to be modelled. Double exponential smoothing includes an additional smoothing parameter for the trend: β. Again the smoothing parameter can vary from 0 to 1.

Triple exponential smoothing extends the double exponential smoothing to allow for seasonal variation. Triple exponential smoothing has three smoothing parameters, with an extra one for the smoothing of the seasonality: α, β, γ. It has an additional parametric for the number of seasons in a year.

The double exponential smoothing and triple exponential smoothing may be calculated with the same library as the simple exponential smoothing example above. In the example given in Box 6.4 triple exponential smoothing is used to predict interest in a 'summer reading challenge'.

Box 6.4 Triple exponential smoothing with Google Trends when predicting interest in a summer reading challenge

Many public libraries around the world hold summer reading challenges to encourage children with their reading. Unsurprisingly many people search for information about these reading challenges, and it has a seasonal pattern (people search for information about summer reading challenges in the summer rather than the winter). Information about these searches can be accessed from Google Trends. It is possible to visit the Google Trends website, enter the required parameters, and save the data as a CSV for analysis, but in this example the data is retrieved directly from the Google Trends website using the gtrendsR library (https://github.com/PMassicotte/gtrendsR):

```
library (gtrendsR)
searches <- gtrends('summer reading challenge', geo = 'GB', time='all')
```

gtrends returns a list of data frames, including interest in different countries, regions and associated topics. This example is specifically interested in the **interest_over_time** data frame. It is necessary to change the format of the date as gtrends dates are of the form yyyy-mm-dd, and the use of day creates irregular intervals (months vary from 28 to 31 days):

```
searchesDF<-data.frame(searches$interest_over_time)
searchesDF$date<- yearmonth(searchesDF$date)
```

The model and forecast may be generated in the same way as for simple exponential smoothing:

```
searchesTS<-as_tsibble(searchesDF, index = date)
fit <- model(searchesTS, ETS(hits))
future <- forecast(fit)
```

As before, the **report()** function may be used to view the parameters of the model. Created automatically, the model has decided on an additive error term, no trend and a seasonal variation. The α parameter is 0.044 and γ is 0.625 (both to 3 d.p.).

Figure 6.2 shows past and forecast data for Google Trends. The shaded area of the graphs show the confidence levels:

```
autoplot(future, searchesTS)
```

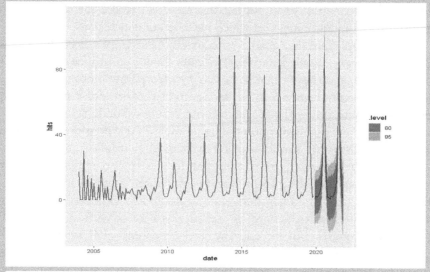

Figure 6.2 *Triple exponential smoothing of past and forecast data on Google Trends*

As with the regression analysis above, this section has taken a rough and ready approach to the application of exponential smoothing, suitable for an initial foray into the topic.

Testing your forecasts

It's very simple to make predictions, the television is full of people making predictions about the future – a particular stock will crash, a war is going to erupt in the Middle East. But the sorts of predictions that keep viewers entertained are not necessarily the most accurate – and although pundits should probably be held accountable for their predictions more often than they are, it is unlikely to make very good television. Data scientists, however, need to take a more robust approach to their forecasts, and are generally more likely to be held to account. A more robust approach includes testing statistical significance, highlighting intervals of confidence, and being wary of overfitting.

The topic of statistical significance has already been touched on a number of times in this book. We cannot simply apply the test multiple times across a data set without taking appropriate measures to account for the increased likelihood of finding a pattern (e.g. Bonferroni correction or Benjamini-Hochberg procedure). We shouldn't tout regression models without ensuring that the underlying coefficients are statistically significant, whether a correlation coefficient for simple linear regression or a multiple correlation coefficient for multiple regression analysis. The web has provided access to vast quantities of data, and statistical lines allow us to generate graphs and equations with just a few lines of code, but it's important that we don't ignore the mathematical and statistical underpinnings on which we base our conclusions.

The same packages that enable us to generate our graphs so easily can also generate a host of detailed statistical insights about significance and intervals of confidence, and these can often easily be incorporated into visualisations (see, for example, Figure 6.2). It is important that we don't just cut-and-paste tables of results without thinking, but ensure we understand what they are telling us, and highlight potential uncertainty in our predictions so that a one-off forecast is not simply labelled 'wrong' when it fails to materialise.

We must be aware of overfitting our results to a particular data set, especially as our modelling techniques become more sophisticated. The cost function, the quantified gap between predicted and expected values (e.g. average squared error), may be reduced to zero with a sufficiently complicated model, but beyond the initial training set it may be totally useless. In machine learning it is typical to distinguish between training sets, validation sets and test sets, and it is important to consider the ramifications of our initial data set for the validity of the models that come from it.

7

Text analysis and mining

As has been seen throughout this book, data is not just numbers but also text, and the internet gives access to vast quantities of text online. This varies from the individual keywords that have been entered into search engines or are associated with bibliographic records, to huge quantities of unstructured text in the form of web pages, blog posts, microblogging updates and articles in online databases. This chapter considers some of the ways this data may be analysed for insights.

Following a brief discussion of how text analysis may be applied by library and information professionals, the chapter is broadly split into two halves. The first half considers natural language processing and the analysis of chunks of text, discussing machine learning, sentiment analysis and topic analysis. The second half considers techniques related to keywords or n-grams; it considers term frequency and burst detection. The two parts are not unrelated; for example keywords may have been extracted through natural language processing or created independently as part of a classification process, whether formal (e.g. applying subject terms) or informal (e.g. tagging).

Text analysis and mining, and information professionals

Of the three approaches to data science considered in this book (clustering and social network analysis, predictions and forecasting, and text analysis and mining), it is probably text analysis that has the most widespread potential for library and information professionals. While each of the approaches has its applications in the library, and there is plenty of overlap (e.g. predictive search suggestions), there are numerous potential applications for text analysis in the library because of the pivotal role of text in the history of the library and driven by the huge growth in online content and unstructured data.

The goal of creating a universal library, which contains all the books and useful information ever published, is ultimately unattainable, but great strides have been taken to achieve it. While the digital revolution has reduced the physical barriers to such a library bringing vast reductions in the costs of digitising, copying and storing publications, there are inevitably certain limitations that will never be overcome: history is filled with lost works; copyright holders may object to their works being deposited in such an online library; and there is a variety of grey literature and unpublished manuscripts that are not included in any library's collection policy. The vast online libraries now available are beyond anything that could be read and analysed by any single individual or group. Even a relatively restrained electronic library like Project Gutenberg (www.gutenberg.org), with its focus on out-of-copyright books, provides free access to over 60,000 books, while the pirate website Sci-Hub (https://sci-hub.tw) claims to provide access to over 76,000,000 research papers, and users of the microblogging site Twitter create over half a billion tweets per day (Twitter, 2013). This vast quantity of resources opens the opportunity for a variety of insights that, while beyond the scope of human readers, may be achieved through computational text analysis.

In contrast to the traditional close reading of literature, this computational text analysis at scale opens the opportunity for 'distant reading' (Moretti, 2013), and with increasing recognition of the economic advantages of AI it has been suggested that the right to read should be the right to mine (Hall and Pesenti, 2017): humanities scholars may identify previously hidden connections across the ages; scientists may mine research papers for undiscovered public knowledge – new insights gleaned from related public knowledge in disparate fields (Swanson, 1986); and marketing executives may gain unexpected insights about public use or opinions of products. Many applications of text analysis have been suggested for library and information professionals. Text mining social media may help library staff understand the most successful content shared by themselves or their users (Al-Daihani and Abrahams, 2016) or explore the trending topics associated with a particular field (Lamba and Madhusudhan, 2018). Topic modelling may be used to help map disciplines (Figuerola, Marco and Pinto, 2017) or to generate metadata automatically (Boman, 2019). Neural networks may form the basis of library discovery systems (Yelton, 2019), and convolutional neural networks have been used to tag a collection of over 1 million book illustrations in the British Library (https://data.bl.uk/research/sherlocknet1.html).

With so much data and so many potential applications available, library and information professionals are only limited in text analysis by their imagination and technical skills. Although there are so many options available it can be difficult to get a purchase point, once you have established a preferred workflow or pipeline for analysing data it can often be easily adapted to examine a whole host of resources and questions with just a few changes.

Natural language processing

The web provides access to various data and resources, but it is the vast quantities of unstructured data available on the web that have driven not only interest in text analysis, but the rise in methodologies that require access to vast quantities of data.

Natural language processing is the use of 'computational techniques for the purpose of learning, understanding, and producing human language content' (Hirschberg and Manning, 2016, 261). In recent years the combination of increasingly large quantities of data with scientific and technological developments has led to the rapid growth of many natural language processing applications: machine translation, spoken dialogue systems, semantic analysis. Many have become quickly adopted by the general public, for example using voice commands to query Siri and Alexa, or translating web pages with Google Translate. Tools for generating content are increasingly widely available, such as Talk to Transformer (https://talktotransformer.com).

Natural language processing technologies have developed and spread so rapidly that it is often easy to overlook their limitations. For example, in the area of language translation, machine translations may translate the gist of a document, but there is still a significant gap in the quality of the translation, and while there are a plethora of tools available for high-resource languages (e.g. English, French, Spanish) there are far fewer, or none, for some low resource languages (e.g. Bengali, Punjabi). As with so many of today's problems, it is hoped that some of these limitations will be overcome with the help of AI.

AI and machine learning

The news is seemingly constantly filled with stories about the impact of AI. On the one hand it is seen as a panacea for all society's ills, improving everything from the NHS (Gallagher, 2019) to the drive-through (BBC News, 2019b) and job satisfaction (Brown, 2019). On the other hand it is going to bring about a dystopian future of racism (Shultes, 2019), fake news (Wakefield, 2019) and joblessness (BBC News, 2019b). The truth is probably somewhere in between. There are opportunities and challenges with AI, although its growing centrality to many companies reflects the fact that future interest in it is likely to increase. It can be seen in Google's decision to rename its research division Google AI (Lunden, 2018) as well as the price commanded by AI researchers from top US universities, reportedly $500,000 a year in their first job (Cellan-Jones, 2017).

The terms artificial intelligence and machine learning are often used interchangeably to refer broadly to the increasing application of computers to tasks that have traditionally been considered the preserve of human intellect. More specifically, machine learning refers to the subset of AI where intelligence is mimicked not through the encoding of explicit rules, but by inferring patterns from large quantities of data that are widely available thanks to the web and the digitisation of our lives. Machine learning is an approach to knowledge discovery, and may be applied in data science, data-driven science, business analytics or data mining. It is often used for natural language processing tasks, but is by no means limited to natural language processing, nor is natural language processing limited to machine learning.

Like so much in the field of data science, the choice of tools available to anyone wanting to use AI are legion. Not only is there a wide variety of software, proprietary and open source, but an increasing number of algorithms that have been developed. Typically machine learning algorithms are classified as supervised or unsupervised, depending on whether the algorithm is trained on a labelled data set (supervised) or extracts patterns on its own (unsupervised). Such a categorisation barely scratches the surface of the variety of algorithms available, and the network of competing, associated and hierarchical relationships between the different terms can quickly leave would-be data scientists overwhelmed. What's the difference between a decision tree, a topic analysis and a neural network? Or a neural network, a deep neural network and a convoluted neural network?

As more algorithms are developed the complexity of the network of associations between algorithms and the labels we apply to them is likely to continue to grow. It is important for information professionals to know that it is not necessary to be proficient in each and every algorithm that emerges, although they should be aware that there are many algorithms that could be used for any particular piece of analysis.

Here we consider just two natural language processing methods: a lexicon approach to sentiment analysis and Latent Dirichlet Allocation for topic analysis, but before looking more closely at the application of these methods, it is worth considering the application of neural networks a bit more closely. Neural networks (and their various subcategories) are one of the most widely used set of approaches to data science, and most clearly illustrate one of the challenges facing data science: the growing gap between the results from AI and our understanding of how it achieved those results.

A neural network, or rather an artificial neural network, is loosely modelled on the neural connections in the human brain, and learns to do specific tasks by analysing numerous examples rather than by being programmed with specific rules. For example, rather than describing what all the versions of the letter 'a' look like for the purposes of character recognition, the neural network is provided with numerous examples. A neural network consists of three layers: input, hidden and output. The input layer is the information gathered for a particular instance. The hidden layer(s) are where the calculation is done with weighted values assigned to channels. The output layer predicts the final output, whether that is an action (e.g. for a self-driving car), a prediction (e.g. for a financial system) or a categorisation (e.g. for a classifier). A deep neural network, enabled by the rapid increase in processing power, has multiple hidden layers. Although we can be sure that neural networks work, as the neural networks get deeper and the problems tackled get more complicated, it is not always clear how they work. Figure 7.1 shows a diagram of a neural network with four inputs, two hidden layers and two possible outputs. There is inevitably a gap between all close and distant reading in understanding how the conclusions are arrived at, and for ever more complex AI algorithms this gap may be insurmountable. This is not merely an intellectual inconvenience, but has important ramifications as AI applications are increasingly rolled out throughout society, and potential biases in the original data are hidden from view. Also, as Yelton (2019) points out, the results produced by neural networks differ from the traditional metadata framework used in library cataloguing and classification: they do not produce definitive categories or subject headings, but rather deal in probabilities and similarities.

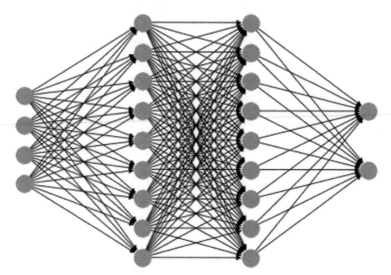

Figure 7.1 *A neural network with four inputs, two hidden layers and two possible outputs*

Sentiment analysis
Sentiment analysis, or opinion mining (the differences are subtle and the terms often used interchangeably), is 'the field of study that analyses people's

opinions, sentiments, appraisals, attitudes, and emotions towards entities and their attributes expressed in written text' (Liu, 2015, 3). There is wide interest in its application because of the large quantity of unstructured text available online, especially on social network sites and sites that solicit user contributions.

There have been sentiment analysis studies on Facebook posts (Al-Daihani and Abrahams, 2018), news articles (Karalevicius, Degrande and De Weerdt, 2018), movie reviews (Hur, Kang and Cho, 2016), TripAdvisor (Valdivia, Luzón and Herrera, 2017) and Amazon.com (Fang and Zhan, 2015). In a bibliometric analysis Mäntylä, Graziotin and Kuutila (2018) found that there has been a shift in recent years away from product reviews to social media texts and extending sentiment analysis to a far wider range of topics. Many research studies have focused on Twitter because of its association with current events ('What's happening?' it asks) and as it originally had an extensive set of APIs and was open by default. Within the library community sentiment analysis has been used on academic library tweets (Al-Daihani and Abrahams, 2016; Stewart and Walker, 2018), academic library Facebook posts (Al-Daihani and Abrahams, 2018) and to explore tweets on topics of interest to a subject librarian (Lamba and Madhusudhan, 2018).

Various sentiment analysis tools are available, from downloadable desktop software (e.g. GATE, https://gate.ac.uk) to web services (e.g. Microsoft Azure Text Analytics, https://azure.microsoft.com/en-gb/services/cognitive-services/text-analytics), from lexicon approaches (e.g. AFINN, https://github.com/fnielsen/afinn) to machine learning approaches (e.g. the tone analyser of IBM Watson, of *Jeopardy!* winning fame, https://www.ibm.com/watson/developer), from tools that are solely for sentiment analysis (e.g. SentiStrength, http://sentistrength.wlv.ac.uk) to those that are part of a wider natural language processing framework (e.g. Stanford CoreNLP, https://stanfordnlp.github.io/CoreNLP) and from those that are free (e.g. LightSide, http://ankara.lti.cs.cmu.edu/side) to those that cost (e.g. AYLIEN, https://aylien.com/text-api) – albeit often with a level of freemium functionality. Sentiment analysis is a popular and dynamic area of research, and the community shows few signs of coalescing around any particular tool. As always, selection is liable to be built on resources available, as well as previous experience.

In the example demonstrated in Box 7.1 and Figure 7.2 opposite a lexicon approach is taken to sentiment analysis using R. There are many sentiment packages available for R: syuzhet (https://github.com/mjockers/syuzhet) incorporates multiple different lexicons, sentimentr (https://github.com/trinker/sentimentr) incorporates weightings for valence shifters (words like 'not', 'very' or 'hardly'), and the text mining package quanteda (https://quanteda.io) allows natural language processing supervised learning sentiment analysis. It is simple to apply syuzhet, which is used in the example below to analyse the 500 most recent tweets with the hashtag #brexit.

Box 7.1 #Brexit sentiment analysis

This example uses data from Twitter, and the notebook is available at https://github.com/dpstuart/jupyter. The sentiment analysis uses three libraries: **rtweet** for simple interaction with the Twitter API, **syuzhet** (https://github.com/mjockers/syuzhet) for the sentiment analysis, and **ggplot2** (https://ggplot2.tidyverse.org/) for the visualisation:

```
library(rtweet)
library(syuzhet)
library(ggplot2)
```

Unlike the other examples in the book the Twitter API requires authentication, and to run the example it is necessary to sign up for a developer account, create an 'app', and generate the necessary keys and tokens (https://developer.twitter.com). These keys are then used to generate a token for interacting with the API (see https://rtweet.info/articles/auth.html for further details):

```
# XXXXXX's should be replaced by your own app details
appname = 'XXXXXX'
key='XXXXXX'
secret = 'XXXXXX'
access_token= 'XXXXXX'
access_secret= 'XXXXXX'

twitter_token <- create_token(
        app = appname,
        consumer_key = key,
        consumer_secret = secret,
        access_token = access_token,
        access_secret = access_secret)
```

Once the application has been authenticated, data can be downloaded into a data frame with a single line of code using the **search_tweets()** function, in this case the 500 most recent tweets with the hashtag #Brexit:

```
brxTwts <- search_tweets(q = "#Brexit", n = 500)
```

The **$text** of the tweets contains a lot of information that you may want to exclude from the sentiment analysis, for example, emoji, hashtags, usernames and URI links. The code below strips out each in turn. The **iconv()** function converts the text from the original encoding which allows emoji (latin1) to one that doesn't (ASCII). The **gsub()** function uses regular expression pattern matching to replace matching code with a replacement value (in this case an empty string):

```
brxTwts$plaintext <- sapply(brxTwts$text,function(x)
        iconv(x, 'latin1', 'ASCII', sub="))
brxTwts$plaintext <- apply(brxTwts[, 'plaintext'], 1, function(x) {
        gsub('#\\S+', ", x)})
brxTwts$plaintext <- apply(brxTwts[, 'plaintext'], 1, function(x) {
        gsub('@\\S+', ", x)})
brxTwts$plaintext <- apply(brxTwts[, 'plaintext'], 1, function(x) {
        gsub("https://[[:graph:]]*",' ', x)})
```

Each of the cleaned tweets is now split into sentences **get_sentences()**, for each of which the sentiment is calculated using the syuzhet method (**get_sentiment()**), and then totalled for the tweet and stored in a new **$syuzhet** column:

```
brxTwts$syuzhet <- apply(brxTwts[, 'plaintext'], 1, function(x){
        sum(get_sentiment(get_sentences(x), method= "syuzhet")) } )
```

The table may then be reordered according to the syuzhet value, and the results shown in a rank order graph (see Figure 7.2):

```
brxTwts <- brxTwts[order(brxTwts$syuzhet),]
ggplot(data= brxTwts, aes(x=as.numeric(row.names(brxTwts)),
                y= brxTwts $syuzhet))+
    geom_bar(stat='identity') + xlab(' ') + ylab('Brexit Sentiment')
```

Figure 7.2 shows clearly that Brexit is a divisive subject, with almost 200 of the tweets having a negative sentiment, and a little over 200 having a positive sentiment. It is important, however, to see this in the context of other data samples. Have the proportions changed over time? Is it more divisive than other topics? Are the sentiments expressed more strongly than for other issues?

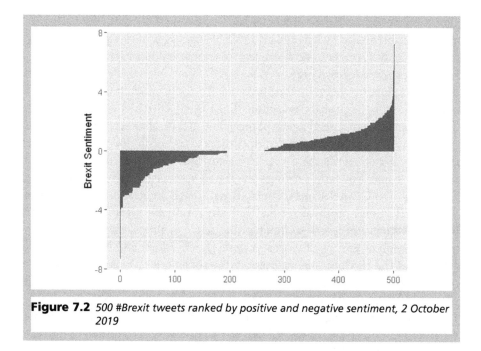

Figure 7.2 *500 #Brexit tweets ranked by positive and negative sentiment, 2 October 2019*

The main limitation of lexicon-based approaches is their ability to deal adequately with domain and context specific 'orientations' (Serrano-Guerrero et al., 2015), and an increasing number of studies use deep learning approaches (Zhang, Wang and Liu, 2018). There are inevitable difficulties in identifying sentiment in certain texts for both approaches (especially where sarcasm is involved) whether you are human or machine (González-Ibáñez, Muresan and Wacholder, 2011).

Topic modelling

Topic modelling is another natural language processing methodology, which is used to discover a 'hidden thematic structure in large collections of texts' (Blei, 2012). It may be thought of as a clustering algorithm, suitable for large sets of documents, but whereas the k-means clustering algorithm (introduced in Chapter 5) has items assigned to just one cluster, with topic modelling multiple topics may be assigned to each document.

Topic modelling uses text mining to identify the 'topics', patterns of co-occurring words, in a corpus of documents (Brett, 2012). It has been used for mapping many different fields and disciplines, including library science (Figuerola, Marco and Pinto, 2017), and to analyse a wide variety of document types, from scientific abstracts (Figuerola, Marco and Pinto, 2017) to poetry (Rhody, 2012). Importantly, from the perspective of resource allocation, topic modelling processes such as Latent Dirichlet Allocation can easily be implemented with publicly available packages in R (e.g. topicmodels, https://CRAN.R-project.org/package=topicmodels) and Python (e.g. scikit-learn, https://scikit-learn.org).

The simplest of the various approaches to topic modelling, and the one applied here, is the probabilistic modelling Latent Dirichlet Allocation (Blei, 2012). It makes two broad assumptions (Blei, 2012): there are many patterns of word use, topics, that occur in documents, and each document varies in the extent it represents the topic. The algorithm doesn't return a label for a particular topic, but rather returns the terms associated with the topic. In a good topic model the terms associated with each topic should make sense (Brett, 2012) and produce results that are actionable (Rhody, 2012). The problem is that words 'are so flexible that one can almost always provide an interpretation of groups of words *ex post*' (Leydesdorff and Nerghes, 2017, 1026), and the random starting point in the technique means two runs don't necessarily produce the same results and you can run the model multiple times until a satisfying answer is achieved (Leydesdorff and Nerghes, 2017, 1034). Topic modelling is best viewed as a tool for exploration rather than a provider of definitive answers; it is a tool for discovery rather than to provide evidence (Brett, 2012).

Latent Dirichlet Allocation has been applied to many data types: abstracts of peer-reviewed publications (Figuerola, Marco and Pinto, 2017), doctoral theses (Sugimoto et al., 2011), e-petitions (Hagen, 2018) and Twitter (Karami and Collins, 2019). It has even been used to explore topics in poetry, although it has been suggested that the analysis of poetry doesn't work in the same way as for science: 'topic keyword distributions in a thematic light appear at first glance to be riddled with "intrusions"' (Rhody, 2012). This re-emphasises the point that topic modelling is primarily a tool for exploration rather than to find definitive answers, and when viewed in this light it has been suggested that even when it fails it can 'fail in ways that are potentially productive for literary scholars' (Rhody, 2012).

More specifically, library and information professionals have used Latent Dirichlet Allocation to analyse the topic of library posts on Twitter (Karami and Collins, 2019) and the dominant topics of library and information science doctoral theses (Sugimoto et al., 2011). Boman (2019) attempted a Latent Dirichlet Allocation approach to the generation of subject topics for books on Project Gutenberg, although his suggestion that a Latent Dirichlet Allocation approach to topic modelling in libraries 'should allow machine learning librarians to determine the aboutness of a resource approximating the application of official library subject headings' (Boman, 2019, 23) is probably a step too far. It may extend the depth and breadth of catalogues and discovery services, but as Boman (2019) points out, we can't expect it to solve the problem of bias in the library.

In Box 7.2 topic modelling is used to explore the topics of articles in the preprint repository arXiv (https://arxiv.org).

Box 7.2 The use of topic modelling to explore the topics of articles in the preprint repository arXiv

This example uses data from the arXiv preprint repository, and the code is available at https://github.com/dpstuart/jupyter. The data is accessed using the aRxiv library (https://github.com/ropensci/aRxiv), specifically designed for interaction with the arXiv API, transformed and cleaned with the text mining library tm (http://tm.r-forge.r-project.org), and then explored with the topicmodels library (https://cran.r-project.org/web/packages/topicmodels):

```
library(aRxiv)
library(tm)
library(topicmodels)
```

The arXiv API doesn't require any authentication, so it is a straightforward process to download the records into a data frame and then use the abstract column as the basis for the corpus for analysis. In this case the first 1000 records with the category code for digital libraries (cs.DL) are downloaded:

```
arxivDF <- arxiv_search('cat:cs.DL', limit=1000)
```

The **$abstract** field from the data frame is transformed into a corpus using the **Corpus()** function from the **tm** library (written in full as there is also a **corpus()** function in the **topicmodels** library used below). It is then transformed using the **tm_map()** function to clean the data: standardising capitalisation and removing punctuation, numbers, white spaces and stop words:

```
corpus <- tm::Corpus(VectorSource(as.vector(arxivDF$abstract)))
corpus <- tm_map(corpus,content_transformer(tolower))
corpus <- tm_map(corpus, removePunctuation)
corpus <- tm_map(corpus, removeNumbers)
corpus <- tm_map(corpus, stripWhitespace)
corpus <- tm_map(corpus, removeWords, stopwords("english"))
```

The cleaned corpus is then used to create a document term matrix that can be passed to the **LDA()** function. Along with the number of topics that are required, it is necessary to provide the method, a choice of Gibbs or variational expectation maximisation (VEM). It is possible to provide control through a list containing the Dirichlet prior alpha and Dirichlet prior beta; these may be thought of as the tuning of the model. A higher alpha indicates a larger number of topics per document, whereas a higher beta indicates a higher number of words per topic. This example uses the default values:

```
dtm <- tm::DocumentTermMatrix(corpus)
T = 4 # number of topics
alpha = 50/T # dirichlet prior alpha
beta = 0.1 # dirichlet prior beta
model = topicmodels::LDA(dtm,
                    k = T,
                    method = 'Gibbs',
                    control = list(alpha=alpha,
                                delta=beta))
print(as.matrix(terms(model,10)))
```

The results of the top ten terms for four topics can be seen in Table 7.1. We might conceivably propose to label them: 'information systems and modelling' (Topic 1), 'digital libraries and open access' (Topic 2), 'scientific networks' (Topic 3) and 'bibliometrics' (Topic 4). The validity of these topics to describe the contents of the articles categorised as digital libraries in the arXiv would require further exploration though. We might like to explore what happens if we exclude more stop words (e.g. 'can' and 'two'), use the stems of words (e.g. 'use', 'users', 'used' and 'using') or increase the number of topics.

Table 7.1 *The results of the top ten terms for four topics in digital libraries*

Topic 1	Topic 2	Topic 3	Topic 4
'information', 'system', 'paper', 'use', 'systems', 'search', 'users', 'can', 'model', 'used'	'data', 'web', 'digital', 'open', 'access', 'will', 'resources', 'content', 'library', 'community'	'research', 'scientific', 'science', 'can', 'analysis', 'different', 'network', 'knowledge', 'study', 'using'	'citation', 'journals', 'papers', 'impact', 'journal', 'number', 'citations', 'articles', 'authors', 'two'

Like many of the data tools mentioned in this book, topic modelling is not a panacea for all a library's problems in a world increasingly suffering from information overload, but provides a new way of exploring some of the vast quantities of data that are now beyond the scope of a single individual to read. Latent Dirichlet Allocation is undoubtedly one of the more accessible of the machine learning algorithms, and although we should heed Leydesdorff and Nerghes' (2017, 1034) assessment that the increased availability of topic modelling tools invites 'use without further reflection', it is essential that librarians are aware of and play with the tools available while keeping their limitations in mind.

Keywords and n-grams

Not all text analysis necessitates natural language processing. The web is filled with sources of structured text (e.g. Google Trends, Wikidata), unstructured text that has already been parsed by an external service (e.g. Google Ngram Viewer), as well as a host of unstructured text where the words do not need to be explored for meaning, but where the individual words may be considered in isolation, rather than looking for any particular underlying meaning.

Unlike much of the work of natural language processing and machine learning, where the working of algorithms can be obscured from users, keyword and term analysis is far more explicit. For example, using data from Google Trends we can say that 'machine learning' became a more popular search term than 'artificial intelligence' in the US in June 2013. This is an objective transparent quantifiable assessment that is simple to understand (Figure 7.3). The y-axis represents search interest relative to the highest point on the graph. That doesn't mean the comparison is beyond criticism, in fact it is more open to criticism because the assertions being made are so much clearer. It may be that 'machine learning' overtook 'artificial intelligence' later if we bundle umbers of results for 'artificial intelligence' with those for AI, or we might argue that Google data does not reflect wider search trends, or that there are limitations in the Google Trends tool.

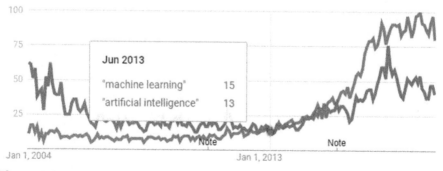

Figure 7.3 *Use of 'machine learning' and 'artificial intelligence' in the US measured on Google Trends, 2004–13;* Google and the Google logo are registered trademarks of Google Inc., used with permission

The point is that there is something explicit to argue against.

In this section we consider frequency and burst detection. Frequency of terms (or strings of terms – n-grams) are often used to show the dominance or growth of one particular set of terms rather than others.

Term frequency

At its simplest level, text analysis may use the frequency of a term as an indicator of the importance of an underlying concept to a document or a corpus of documents. The idea that a document about giraffes will at some point in the text mention the term 'giraffe' forms the backbone of much information retrieval. It is not the only indicator of a document's relevance, and other surrounding texts may provide insights, but the difference between the appearance of a term in a text and non-appearance is often fundamental to its retrieval.

The reliance on any indicator is quickly open to abuse, especially when there is little control of the documents in a particular corpus. On the web, for example, the keyword stuffing of early web pages to increase the chances of retrieval by search engines meant that the frequency-based algorithms were far inferior to the network-based algorithm of Google, which quickly gained market dominance. However, Google itself is by no means immune to the problem of manipulation: the use of anchor text to provide insights into the underlying concepts of a linked-to document led to many infamous cases of Google bombing, for example, where the search for 'miserable failure' returned the web page for the then president George W. Bush.

From a data science perspective, interest is less in the retrieval of documents and more in the insights that can be gleaned from a corpus of documents. Frequency can provide insights into not only how terms appear within different corpora of documents, but also how the frequency changes over time. Although the study of n-grams, the appearance of a series of characters (typically a series of words), has an established history within computational linguistics, it gained widespread attention with the advent of Google Books Ngram Viewer, allowing for the simple historical exploration of how phrases have appeared in Google's corpus of digitised books. Since the Google Books Ngram Viewer was released in 2010, it has been incorporated into many academic studies in various fields. For example, it has been used to explore the rise in individualistic words and phrases (Twenge, Campbell and Gentile, 2012) and pronouns (Twenge, Campbell and Gentile, 2013) in books, the reflection of inflation and unemployment rates in the sentiment of books (a 'literary misery index') (Bentley et al., 2014) and interest in the environmental issues in the past (Richards, 2013).

It is important to be aware of the limitations and biases that any data source incorporates. For example, Pechenick, Danforth and Dodds (2015) note that as Google Books only includes one copy of each book, and gives no indication of whether a book is widely read or not, obscure but prolific authors may have an undue influence on the corpus. Equally the proportion of scientific literature that makes up the corpus in the 20th century can skew the findings (Pechenick, Danforth and Dodds, 2015). Pettit (2016) points out, among other criticisms, that print culture does not necessarily represent the whole of a culture, and word meanings change over time.

Such general corpora still have their uses, but there is a need to be aware of a tool's limitations. Several other n-gram viewers and data sets have been made available for other more specialised collections, for example, the n-gram viewer for Dutch newspapers 1840–1995 (https://lab.kb.nl/tool/newspaper-ngram-viewer) and television news n-gram data sets (https://blog.gdeltproject.org/announcing-the-television-news-ngram-datasets-tv-ngram).

N-grams have also formed the basis of analysis in the library and information sector. Al-Daihani and Abrahams used unigrams, bigrams and trigrams as part of an analysis of Twitter updates by academic libraries on Twitter (Al-Daihani and Abrahams, 2016) and Facebook posts by academic libraries (Al-Daihani and Abrahams, 2018).

As is increasingly the case for most types of data science, there are many libraries available for those who want to explore the frequency of terms and n-grams in their own data set: TextBlob (https://textblob.readthedocs.io) is a natural language processing library for Python that allows n-grams analysis, while quanteda (https://quanteda.io) provides similar functionality for R. quanteda (https://quanteda.io) is used in the example in Box 7.3 to explore the unigrams and 4-grams of digital library articles in the preprint repository arXiv (https://arxiv.org).

Box 7.3 How to find the most frequently used terms in articles on digital libraries in arXiv

Continuing with the arXivDF data frame from the topic modelling example described in Box 7.2, this time data is analysed with quanteda (https://quanteda.io). The ggplot2 (https://ggplot2.tidyverse.org) data visualisation package is used to visualise the n-grams in a bar chart:

```
library(quanteda)
library(ggplot2)
```

Once again, the abstract column forms the basis of the corpus, and the **corpus()** function from the quanteda library is used to transform the abstracts into a corpus object:

```
absCorp <- quanteda::corpus(arxivDF$abstract)
```

The corpus of abstracts can be turned into a document-feature matrix with the **dfm()** function, which (after removing stop words and punctuation) can simply show the most frequently used terms in the corpus. In this example the top 20 results are returned using the **topfeatures()** function (see Table 7.2).

```
absDFM<-dfm(absCorp, remove = stopwords('english'),
          remove_punct = TRUE)
topfeatures(absDFM, 20)
```

Table 7.2 *The 20 most frequently used terms in abstracts on digital libraries in arXiv, September 2019*

Term	Frequency	Term	Frequency	Term	Frequency
data	918	science	439	using	314
citation	604	web	434	new	303
can	561	journals	366	different	298
research	534	papers	356	analysis	293
information	500	system	332	journal	292
paper	480	impact	326	results	288
scientific	449	based	325		

The most frequently used terms may be simply shown as a word cloud (Figure 7.4): textplot_wordcloud(absDFM, max_words=100)

Figure 7.4 *An arXiv word cloud for abstracts on digital libraries, September 2019*

Box 7.4 N-grams in articles on digital libraries in arXiv

The **tokens()** function in quanteda can be used to change how the corpus is tokenised, how the document is split into smaller pieces of text. By default the text is analysed as unigrams, in this case its text is tokenised as 4-grams, although it could just as easily be analysed as bigrams (**ngrams=2**), trigrams (**ngrams=3**) or multiple-sized n-grams (e.g. **ngrams=3:4**). Once again the **dfm()** function creates the document-feature matrix so the 20 most frequent n-grams can be identified with the **topfeatures()** function:

```
absToks<-tokens(absCorp, ngrams=4, concatenator = ' ',
                remove_numbers=TRUE, remove_punct=TRUE)
absNgrams<-topfeatures(dfm(absToks), n=20)
```

This time the most frequent phrases are transformed into a data frame, which is then used to display the most frequent 4-grams (see Figure 7.5):

```
ngramDF<-as.data.frame(absNgrams)
ggplot(ngramDF, aes(x=reorder(row.names(ngramDF),
       ngramDF$absNgrams), y=ngramDF$absNgrams) )+
       geom_bar(stat='identity')+ coord_flip()
       + xlab('4-grams') + ylab('Count')
```

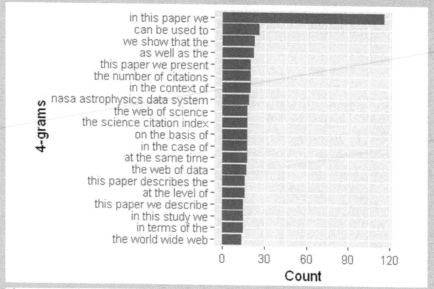

Figure 7.5 *The most frequent 4-grams in articles on digital libraries in arXiv, September 2019*

Perhaps unsurprisingly, such a large number of terms in each sequence (four) means that the list is dominated by common place phrases and proper nouns consisting of multiple words.

Burst detection

It is not always enough just to spot the most popular terms, you may want to identify the trending terms. More useful than knowing that Trump is frequently mentioned is knowing that he is more frequently mentioned than usual, or a little known politician who is hardly mentioned has suddenly been mentioned dozens of times in a short period of time. The little known politician may still not have been mentioned as often as Trump over the same period, but the little known politician is nonetheless noteworthy. One way of identifying these emerging trends in real time is to use Kleinberg's burst detection algorithm (Kleinberg, 2003), which identifies the burst of topics within a temporal stream of documents. Burst detection and variations on the idea have been applied to several document types: link creation in blogs (Kumar et al., 2005), events on Twitter (Weng and Lee, 2011), spam reviews (Xie et al., 2012) and topics in research papers (Pollack and Adler, 2015).

Within the library it is simple to imagine how a burst analysis might be applied to gain insight into the changing information environment. It might include tracking emerging topics discussed by libraries on Twitter, or the subjects of the books borrowed by a library's patron. Box 7.5 applies a burst analysis to the topic 'data science', once again using data from the arXiv repository.

Box 7.5 A burst analysis of the term 'data science' in arXiv

This example uses data from the arXiv repository using the aRxiv library (https://github.com/ropensci/aRxiv) and analyses it with the bursts library (https://cran.r-project.org/web/packages/bursts), which is specifically designed for analysing bursts using the Kleinberg algorithm:

```
library(aRxiv)
library(bursts)
```

arXiv records where the abstract includes the phrase 'data science' are stored in the data frame arxivDf:

```
arxivDF <- arxiv_search('abs:"data science"', limit=1000)
```

The **kleinberg()** function is used to analyse the dates when documents were submitted to the repository, and identify any bursts in the submission data. The function accepts arguments *s* and *gamma*. An increase in *s* increases the intensity that is necessary to be considered a burst, and higher *gamma* values increase the length of time a burst must be sustained. It should be noted that the algorithm won't work if two events occur at the same time, so additional cleaning or wrangling may be necessary:

```
bursts<-kleinberg(as.POSIXct(arxivDF$submitted))
```

The **bursts** object contains a list of the bursts: the level, the start date and the end date. This data can be simply plotted with the **plot()** function:

```
#accumulation of submissions
plot(as.POSIXct(arxivDF$submitted),1:length(as.POSIXct(arxivDF$submitted)),
    xlab='Time', ylab='Submissions')

#bursts in submissions
plot(bursts, xaxt = 'n')
axis.POSIXct(1, bursts$start)
```

Figure 7.6 shows the accumulation of 'data science' submissions to the repository (on the left) and the bursts in submissions (on the right). Level 1 represents the time of the first event to the time of the last, the additional levels represent the bursts.

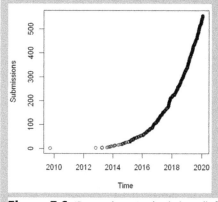 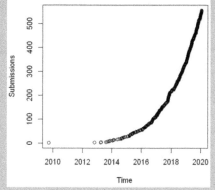

Figure 7.6 *'Data science' submissions (left) and bursts in submissions (right) to the arXiv repository, 2010–20*

The future of data science and information professionals

This final chapter considers the future growth of data science and the role of information professionals as they continue to reposition themselves in the changing information ecosystem. Short of a worldwide catastrophe, it is impossible to see anything but the continued rapid growth of data over the coming years. Whatever measure is used, data production and consumption is expected to rise. For example, the Computer Information System Company (Cisco) predicts that by 2022 there will be more internet traffic per year than there was between 1984 and 2016 (Cooney, 2018).

The way particular sets of data are able to be used will differ. With the introduction of the GDPR access to personal data is already restricted, but whether we are talking big data, little data or some as yet unheralded type of data – there will be more data and more data science.

This growth will be accompanied by many opportunities for data science in the sciences, arts and humanities, as well as in homes, offices, businesses and of course libraries. Data science work has been described as the 'sexiest job of the 21st century' (Davenport and Patil, 2012), and while that is a description that is rarely levelled at library and information professionals, this book should have helped to persuade readers that there are opportunities for library and information professionals to help others apply data science methods, and to use data science methodologies in their own work.

This chapter consists of three parts:

- a list of eight challenges facing data science; although it is a field in the ascendency, associated with progress and all things modern, it is essential that we are aware of some of the challenges data science continues to face, and don't get caught up in the more extreme hyperbole of the hype cycle
- a list of ten steps that would-be library and information science professionals might take when embarking on a career in data science librarianship; as has been frequently expressed throughout this book, a

lot falls under the data science umbrella, and the practical first steps are all too easily overlooked

- a short call to play; there is no book or course that can give more than the most basic of introductions to data science. As discussed in the opening chapter, data science sits at the intersection of domain expertise, mathematical and statistical knowledge, and coding and hacking skills, and the only way any practitioner can get to grips with the many different tools, technologies and data now available is to begin to play with them.

Eight challenges to data science

Many challenges face the adoption of data science methodologies, and library and information professionals are ideally situated to help overcome many of them.

1 Data literacy

Data literacy is 'a specific skill set and knowledge base, which empowers individuals to transform data into information and into actionable knowledge by enabling them to access, interpret, critically assess, manage, and ethically use data' (Koltay, 2017, 10). By this stage of the book, after considering some of the many different tools, data sets and methodologies available, it is probably quite clear that most people may be considered data illiterate. Even implementing neural networks in a library discovery system may require consideration of users' data literacy, as the users may not know how to interpret the results they are shown properly, often assigning too much authority to them (Yelton, 2019).

Data literacy requires a broad range of skills that is constantly evolving in line with technical, environmental and scholarly factors, and it is unreasonable to expect every individual in an organisation to keep on top of the changing landscape on their own. New tools, laws and scholarly practices all require regular updating of the skill set required to understand them, and librarians' expertise and information skills make them ideal contenders to provide instruction (Federer, Lu and Joubert, 2016).

2 Data discovery

Before data can be transformed into information and actionable knowledge, the data itself must be identified, and as has been reiterated throughout this book, it can be problematic to identify data because of the limitations in the tools available for finding data and the data itself: there is no single one-stop shop for data searching, and data often has poor metadata.

In many ways it is as though we are still at the stage of a pre-Google web of documents. Far too much browsing and serendipity is currently required when finding data. Undoubtedly things are beginning to change: researchers are increasingly aware of the importance of sharing data, and the need for quality metadata; organisations are aware of the need to support researchers in making their data available in the best way possible; and data discovery services are being developed. There is still a long way to go, however, in ensuring that data adheres to FAIR principles (is findable, accessible, interoperable, reusable), and information professionals have an important contribution to make.

3 Tool management

Successful data scientists need to keep on top of not only the increasing quantities of data, but the vast numbers of tools now available. Dozens of tools and libraries have been mentioned throughout this book, but they are not even the tip of the data science iceberg: new tools emerge all the time, as does new functionality for existing tools.

Understanding all the intricacies of some of the more complex tools or software libraries may take years to master, yet often librarians as data scientists want to do a smash-and-grab, using a single algorithm or function as a one off. It is unrealistic to expect to be an expert in all the tools you probably want to use, rather you need to rely on online communities of practice and focus on developing expertise in the few key tools and libraries you use most often.

4 Data privacy and security

The growth of data and data science raises numerous legal and ethical issues. For the most part these have been eschewed in this book, which has focused on the practical side of data science, but failure to adhere to the growing amount of legislation surrounding data can have very serious practical consequences for library and information professionals.

During the writing of this book privacy and ethics have increasingly become the subject of public conversation as society weighs up the competing claims to personal data. It is an area where there are no simple answers – reducing access to certain data sources may help to protect personal privacy, but may restrict a researcher's ability to make new discoveries, or our ability to receive innovative new services, whether helping us get our shopping a little quicker or identifying medical risks factors.

However careful we may try to be with data, we nonetheless inevitably have less privacy than we presume. In 2007 it was reported that anonymised

Netflix users could be identified through cross-referencing with IMDB data (Demerjian, 2007); only four spatio-temporal points of mobile phone use were found to be needed to identify 95% of individuals (Montjoye et al., 2013); and even if you are careful with your personal data others may not be. For example, predictions about your predisposition to health complications may be informed by close relatives choosing to have their own DNA tested.

There is an ongoing debate about how we deal with personal data, and the information community has an important role to play in advocacy and education.

5 Algorithmic accountability

Related to the ethics surrounding data privacy and security is the idea of algorithmic accountability. Having accountability means taking responsibility for processes and decisions made, although it's not always simple to decide who should be accountable, and regulation frameworks are struggling to keep up with the rapidly changing environment (House of Commons Science and Technology Committee, 2018).

The datafication of ever growing amounts of people's lives provides greater opportunities for decision-making responsibilities to be taken by a machine rather than a person. This is not only about the ads that follow you around the web, algorithms may have an impact on job appointments, mortgage decisions or even whether you achieve parole, and the workings of the algorithm may be a trade secret (Martin, 2018). It is important, therefore, that someone is held responsible for the decision of the algorithm. Just because you have the right to use data, doesn't mean you should have the right to base decisions on that data, especially where it can be a self-perpetuating cycle, dismissing already marginalised communities.

However much data is collected, it never reflects the complexity of a whole person, which can lead to people being 'pigeon holed . . . based on probability not reality' (Marr, 2015, 151). Of primary concern is the fear that crude generalisations can lead to the perpetuation of racist or sexist discrimination, but it is important to recognise that we are not the same person at all times, or in all situations. For example, while former president of the US Bill Clinton was generally trusted not to start a nuclear war, people were probably less likely to trust him with the office intern. It is important that algorithm accountability doesn't blur the lines to the extent that only one crude reflection of a person is allowed to exist.

6 Understanding the black box

Accompanying the challenge of individuals and organisations being accountable for the algorithms that they use is the challenge of understanding how the algorithms work. We are adopting ever more algorithms in decision making and making greater use of the AI underpinning those algorithms, so users of the algorithm can find it increasingly difficult, if not impossible, to understand on what basis decisions are being made. While legislation may restrict algorithms being used in the realm of personal information, there are many other situations where we are gradually losing sight of what is going on in the black box. For example, in automated trading on the stock exchange there are increasingly complex algorithms, which are interacting with other algorithms in the marketplace with unforeseen consequences (Lange, Lenglet and Seyfert, 2016).

One way to deem the appropriateness of the algorithm is by its results. If the results go in the face of all intuition, then the algorithm is probably wrong. Unfortunately if it's already wiped billions of dollars off of the stock market by that point, or even a trillion dollars in the case of the 'Flash Crash' of 2010 (Lange, Lenglet and Seyfert, 2016), or led to a nuclear meltdown, then 'wait and see' is probably not the best failsafe design.

7 Developing new algorithms

The developments in data science are awe inspiring, but that shouldn't blind us to the fact that there is still a long way to go. If we are to discover useful needles in the ever increasing number of haystacks of data, especially meaningful data in real time, new algorithms need to be created. The application of tools like AlphaZero in a controlled universe, where the program learned and surpassed hundreds of years of chess knowledge in just four hours (Knapton and Watson, 2017), should not blind us to the challenges of the complex and messy world of data science in the real world. These challenges range from autonomous vehicles struggling with adverse weather conditions (Zang et al., 2019) to the problem of matching similarly named items in bibliographic databases. In some cases the problems may require a host of scientific developments and innovations to be overcome, in others simply the allocation of greater resources.

When considering future developments and limitation of data science, and AI in particular, it is worth keeping in mind Arthur C. Clarke's first law: 'When a distinguished but elderly scientist states that something is possible, (s)he is almost certainly right. When (s)he states that something is impossible, (s)he is very probably wrong' (Clarke, 1999, 2).

Whatever you consider beyond the resources of today, may be noted for tomorrow: real-time analysis, massive quantities of data, or no data at all. All may be overcome by new data sources, new algorithms, new laws or the potential of new quantum computers.

8 Data hype cycle

Finally data science must face the realities of the hype cycle. The development of any new technology is inevitably followed by pundits first extolling its potential, and then its failings. Although the library and information science community may be better placed than most to evaluate new technologies, its members are nonetheless subject to the same hype cycle as everybody else, being accused of tending 'to fall well within the boundaries of uncritical hype of technologies, and we do not exhibit a critical professional distance from the resources – tending to celebrate rather than evaluate' (Buschman, 2003, 149).

The hype surrounding data can be seen first in its comparison to a new oil, which comparison is increasingly refuted (Rajan, 2017; Sekinah, 2019). Of course all metaphors break down eventually, but the data-oil comparison breaks remarkably quickly. The potential value that can come from some of the vast quantities of data that is now available is not in doubt, but realising the value of that data is not always as simple as digging a hole in the ground and extracting something that is sitting waiting to be tapped. Although there are undoubtedly powerful data monopolies (the so-called gang of four: Facebook, Google, Amazon and Apple) that control vast quantities of data, there are countless other organisations that may use data science. The analogy is more akin to the application of oil to various machinery, rather than being the process of digging it out of the ground. Data science may be a long term undertaking, with the data not yet ready to exploit, so like oil, but where we are in the Jurassic Age and the plankton has just sunk to the bottom of the ocean. Data science may require the bringing together of a host of different resources, having more in common with a national electricity grid drawing on multiple different energy resources to provide electricity, rather than simply oil. The most important difference is that data, like all information, is a non-depletable resource: if one person is using a data resource, it is nonetheless still there for use by others.

Increased recognition of the limitations of data science is to be welcomed, especially increased recognition of the quantification fallacy. This is where flawed decision making occurs through a focus on the quantitative metrics that can be measured and overlooking more qualitative aspects that can't (Kerr and Klonoff, 2019). As well as not getting carried away with the potential of data science, we must not ignore the actual opportunities it brings.

Ten steps to data science librarianship

Having reached this stage of the book library and information professionals should be aware of some of the data, methodologies and tools that are available, and probably already have a few ideas in mind of additional data that may be of interest, and how they may like to use it. However, if you have managed to reach this stage and still are not sure about what to do next with this new found interest, then a few ideas are provided below.

1   Be data savvy

With even the smallest level of engagement with this book, you will have achieved the first stage of data science librarianship: being data savvy. Burton et al. (2018, 7) describe many 'data savvy' roles that surround the world of data scientists: 'Data savvy librarians gain familiarity with the data sets, understand technical methods and techniques, and speak multiple disciplinary languages allowing them to work more closely with researchers or the public.'

It is not necessary to know everything, but there should be an awareness of some of the tools and methods used in data science, and a willingness to engage with them as necessary. Our cognitive bias known as the frequency illusion (also known as the Baader-Meinhoff phenomenon) means that having read this book, data science opportunities are liable to appear everywhere, even if you haven't given data much thought previously.

2   Undertake a data and skills audit

If being data savvy is an awareness and willingness to engage with available data, tools and methodologies, then the natural next step is to take a more structured approach to the process. What are the data and data skills held by the group or organisation? What are the data and data skills needed by the group or organisation? It doesn't even have to be that formal or widespread an audit – it could be limited to carrying out an informal audit of your own data and data skills needs and requirements.

You are inevitably going to find it easier to start on your own data science journey if you focus on the data that is of interest to you. If you are interested in the enquiry desk, then start there; if you are interested in serials, focus on serials.

The Data Skills Audit Toolkit (Jones, Ross and Ruusalepp, 2009) suggests a four stage process for data audit: plan the audit, identify and classify data assets, assess the management of data assets, and report results and recommendations. Planning the audit will depend heavily on the level of management buy-in and formality in the process. As well as defining the scope of the audit, additional planning activities can range from a personal 'to-do' list to the organisation of interviews and establishing a set of questions to ask people. Identifying and classifying data assets not only involves identifying data assets within the scope of the audit, but also classifying them according to their value. Jones, Ross and Ruusalepp (2009) propose three categories for judging the value of data in an organisation's audit: whether it is vital, important or minor. Depending on the nature of the proposed data science audit, an alternative categorisation may be more appropriate, for example, reflecting the suitability or potentiality of the data. Assessing the managing of assets involves gathering more information about the data to determine whether it is being managed appropriately. For example, data may be available but not currently being collected. Reporting the results and recommendations is a necessary part of the ongoing iterative and cyclical nature of the data audit and data science process more widely. The data is being collected so actions can be taken.

Whatever the findings of the data audit, it is important that they feed into the next two suggested steps: advocacy for data science in the library, and advocacy for less data science in the library.

3   Advocate for data science in the library

First, it is important to recognise that if you would like to see a wider application of data science skills in the library but do not have the requisite technical skills yourself, you may still have an important role to play in advocating for the potential of data science in the library. This may be as simple as drawing attention to data opportunities as they occur, promoting the use of data the library already gathers, asking questions about the openness of data in the services the library subscribes to, or looking for new data opportunities the library could benefit from. At a more formal level it may involve initiating a skills audit within the library to determine who within your organisation has the skills to contribute to data science opportunities as they occur, and to promote the sharing and transfer of skills.

There is only so much that can be done ad hoc, and offering a full range of research data services by a library requires either new technologically skilled staff or a great increase in training opportunities for existing staff (Tenopir et al., 2015). New staff or extensive training is likely to require new resources, and advocacy for data science will be required beyond the library to get them. How receptive those with budgetary responsibility are to requests usually depends heavily on the specific case made.

Following a sentiment analysis of Twitter updates in the field of economics, Lamba and Madhusudhan (2018, 8) suggest that a full-time person in a library 'should be assigned to mine all the incoming tweets related to the core subjects dealt with by the library on a daily basis', but obviously it is unrealistic that most library budgets could fund such a post, to do so would probably not be the best use of existing resources, and the proposal is unlikely to lead to a budget increase. Other measures that have a more direct impact on the principal goals of an organisation may be more productive, especially when supported by data science.

As well as trying to increase library budgets, members of the library and information community have an important role to play in informing the wider information environment, petitioning for and responding to public consultations on issues such as copyright and privacy legislation, which establish what can and cannot be done with data and data science tools.

4   Advocate for less data science in the library

It is also important for someone to play devil's advocate. If you're part of an organisation that is well on its way to becoming more data-centric, and is increasingly numbers driven, advocacy may be required to encourage a less data-centric approach to library and information management. The advocate should support the rights of library users to go about their day without being constantly monitored, look at what is not being captured by the metrics, and highlight the limitations of the current algorithms and practices in use.

As Kaplan's law of the instrument puts it, 'Give a small boy a hammer, and he will find that everything he encounters needs pounding' (Kaplan, 1964, 28), and so it is with data science. Data science is a very useful collection of tools, but there is an art to using those tools in the best manner without losing sight of the ultimate goals.

5   Get your hands dirty

Beyond advocacy, there is a need for library and information professionals to get their hands dirty with data, to move from abstract ideas about what is theoretically possible to the complex realities of the real world. Data science is as much an art as a science, and developing the necessary talent requires practice. A data source may have particular idiosyncrasies, or a tool certain limitations, which only become apparent once they are engaged with. The old military adage bears repeating: 'No plan survives contact with the enemy.'

The internet provides the opportunity for you to get your hands dirty from the comfort of your own home, exploring one particular data set of interest to you. There are ever more opportunities for collective explorations through hackathons and data sprints. Hackathons are events where people come together over a short period of time to work on software projects. These may be tech-centric, focusing on a specific technology, or focus-centric, focusing on a specific social or business objective (Briscoe and Mulligan, 2014). Typically hackathons require a level of coding expertise but, especially with focus-centric hackathons, there is a growing interest in reaching beyond the community of coders to include other types of expertise. This increasingly cross-disciplinary physical collocation approach is being applied in more research focused settings, with data sprints applying the ideas of the hackathon to data and research questions (Venturini, Munk and Meunier, 2018).

6   Establish a good enough workflow

Eventually it will be necessary to move away from the collective and explore different data, tools and methodologies for yourself. This book covers many technologies, and is not meant to be prescriptive. Instead it tries to explain the data science process – the workflow or pipeline by which you enact this process. The large number of tools and services available can quickly become overwhelming, a whole mass of competing offerings. The data librarian doesn't just need to be a proficient data wrangler, but a tool wrangler!

> The proliferance of tools and guidance on data science leaves the librarian community overloaded and overwhelmed. . . . Librarians should be able to solve this problem, it is what they do!
>
> (Burton et al., 2018, 10)

The problem of assessing data, tools and services is not as simple as identifying the suitability of a book. The best laid plans and workflows can easily go awry – consider, for example, Boman (2019) who only discovered the need for his data to be in panda data frames after he had spent the time encoding them into JSON files, so he was unable to explore the technology as fully as he had planned.

An important step in this tool wrangling is establishing a pipeline for the data you are interested in that is 'good enough'. Once an initial pipeline has been established it can always be changed to include more data sources, improved data cleaning, new forms of analysis, or alternative methods of communication. Establishing the perfect workflow is impossible with incomplete knowledge of the tools and data available, but we can establish something that is workable and then improve on it. Even the tool we use to frame the problem is liable to have potential room for improvement: we may move from a Microsoft Word document on our desktop, through a Google Doc that multiple participants may contribute to at the same time, to something more formal and bespoke providing the opportunity for structured contributions. Table 8.1 opposite shows some tools that might be used at each stage of the data science workflow.

Eventually experienced data scientists have knowledge and experience of

Table 8.1 *Example of possible tools used for each stage of the data science workflow*

Data science stage	Initial tool
Frame the problem	Microsoft Word
Collect data	TAGS
Transform and clean data	OpenRefine
Analyse data	SentiStrength
Visualise data	RAWGraphs

multiple tools at each of the different stages, and can pick the best route available for the particular task at hand. If there are just three choices at each of the five stages, the number of potential workflows is 243, so even with a relatively limited set of tools we shouldn't expect to identify the best route straight away. The data science process is iterative.

7   Training, training, training

There is a need for improved training for information professionals in data science, from library schools to on-the-job professional training. The need for lifelong learning is now so obvious as to be clichéd in all fields, but this is especially the case where data science is concerned, and new tools and technologies are constantly emerging. It is necessary to learn about not only new tools and libraries, but also new methods and languages as they emerge.

There is currently a perceived skills gap in the library community when addressing data science needs and opportunities, and this is exacerbated when managers don't sufficiently value and incentivise data skills in libraries (Burton et al., 2018). There is currently a credentialing tension between having the necessary skills and being able to demonstrate that you have the necessary skills. This is inevitable in a fast changing field, where the ability to adopt new technologies is probably more important than having initial experience of an established technology, let alone formal qualifications in a particular technology.

Education is not just restricted to self-education, rather it is important that library and information professionals continue in their role as educators, and providing training opportunities for their users.

8   Specialise

Within this book all the different strands of data science have been clumped together. But while wily data scientists may be used to cobbling together different code and using a multitude of software for a wide variety of analysis, growth in data librarianship inevitably allows for a greater amount of specialisation. Hopefully in the future the profession will develop enough for librarians and information professionals to specialise in not just data science but specific aspects of it: text analysis, social network analysis, machine learning, geographic information systems or specific types of data.

This book is a practical introduction to data science, designed to provoke further exploration rather than provide all the answers. Complex subtleties have necessarily been glossed over and defaults accepted with little question. For example, when using Latent Dirichlet Allocation what exactly is the difference between Gibbs and VEM? If you were to change your alpha and beta priors what would you change them to? And how would this be affected by symmetric and asymmetric distribution of the data? These are important questions, but primarily ones of interest to information professionals specialising in topic modelling rather than those who are interested in the vast array of data science methodologies available.

It is important to remember that there is not always one 'correct' answer to a particular question, or from a data set, and various different approaches may produce different insights.

9   Promote

Once you have begun to establish data science services it is time to start demonstrating how they can be applied in and by the library. It is important to demonstrate the successful application of data science to library users and funders, and show the contribution the library can make to a research institute. It is not enough to take a data science approach, you need to show you have taken a data science approach.

The promotion of data science in the library does not necessarily require a large marketing budget, but rather integration into existing engagement activities: promoting data science findings on social media channels, mentioning (where appropriate) data science services at the enquiry desk, or putting up physical exhibits in the library.

10   Push the boundaries

Data science is not standing still, innovation happens all the time, and information professionals have a role to play in making sure they contribute to the pushing of boundaries. Innovation involves developing new tools and algorithms, bringing together new tools and data, and combining tools in multiple different ways. Not just the tools of 'data science' but the tools of library and information management, and information retrieval.

The final word: play

This book has only scraped the surface of what is possible for those interested in the possibilities arising from the increasing quantities of data now available. There are far more tools and techniques that have not been mentioned than those that have.

This book in no way prepares would-be librarians and data scientists with the tools to identify genes associated with a particular disease, make a decision about Euclidean or cosine similarity, or on which to base billion pound investment decisions for a hedge fund, but hopefully it should have provided a sufficient jumping off point for people to start thinking about these decisions themselves. To start dreaming about what is possible, and where they might begin.

If there is one commandment for the would-be data scientist, it is to play. Brett's (2012) comment on topic modelling may be equally applied to data science as a whole: '[It] is complicated and potentially messy but useful and even fun. The best way to understand how it works is to try it.'

It is essential that we keep the human at the centre of this relationship, that we understand the gap between data and reality, and do not become entranced by the numbers. That is what library and information professionals can do better than computer scientists, which is why it is essential that they become more involved in the data science revolution that is occurring.

References

Ackoff, R. L. (1989) From Data to Wisdom, *Journal of Applied Systems Analysis*, **16**, 3–9.

Akoglu, H. (2018) User's Guide to Correlation Coefficients, *Turkish Journal of Emergency Medicine*, **18** (3), 91–3.

Al-Daihani, S. M. and Abrahams, A. (2016) A Text Mining Analysis of Academic Libraries' Tweets, *Journal of Academic Librarianship*, **42**, 135–43.

Al-Daihani, S. M. and Abrahams, A. (2018) Analysis of Academic Libraries' Facebook Posts: text and data analytics, *Journal of Academic Librarianship*, **44**, 216–25.

Almind, T. C. and Ingwersen, P. (1996) Informetric Analysis on the World Wide Web: a methodological approach to 'internetometrics', Centre for Informetric Studies, Royal School of Library and Information Science.

Alpaydin, E. (2016) *Machine Learning*, MIT Press.

Anderson, C. (2008) The End of Theory: the data deluge makes the scientific method obsolete, www.wired.com/science/discoveries/magazine/16-07/pb_theory.

Ball, A. (2014) How to License Research Data, Digital Curation Centre, 17 July, www.dcc.ac.uk/resources/how-guides/license-research-data.

BBC News (2019a) Facebook Users Continue to Grow Despite Privacy Scandals, BBC News, 30 January, https://www.bbc.co.uk/news/business-47065972.

BBC News (2019b) McDonald's Uses AI for Ordering at Drive-throughs, 11 September, https://www.bbc.co.uk/news/technology-49664633.

Bell, G. (2009) Foreword. In Hey, T., Tansley, S. and Tolle, K. (eds), *The Fourth Paradigm: data-intensive scientific discovery*, Microsoft Research.

Bentley, R. A., Acerbi, A., Ormerod, P. and Lampos, V. (2014) Books Average Previous Decade of Economic Misery, *Plos ONE*, https://journals.plos.org/plosone/article?id=10.1371/journal.pone.0083147.

Berman, E. (2018) The Ethics of Privacy in Librarianship, American Library Association, 2 May, https://chooseprivacyeveryday.org/the-ethical-role-of-libraries-and-big-data.

Björneborn, L. and Ingwersen, P. (2004) Toward a Basic Framework for Webometrics, *Journal of the American Society for Information Science and Technology*, **55** (14), 1216–27.

Blei, D. M. (2012) Topic Modeling and Digital Humanities, *Journal of Digital Humanities*, **2** (1), http://journalofdigitalhumanities.org/2-1/topic-modeling-and-digital-humanities-by-david-m-blei.

Boman, C. (2019) An Exploration of Machine Learning in Libraries. In Griffey, J. (ed.), *Artificial Intelligence and Machine Learning in Libraries*, Library Technology Reports, **55** (1), 21–5, https://journals.ala.org/index.php/ltr/issue/view/709.

Borgman, C. L. (2012) The Conundrum of Sharing Research Data, *Journal of the American Society for Information Science and Technology*, **63** (6), 1059–78.

Börner, K. and Polley, D. E. (2014) *Visual Insights: a practical guide to making sense of data*, MIT Press.

Börner, K., Sanyal, S. and Vespignani, A. (2007) Network Science. In Cronin, B. (ed.), *Annual Review of Information Science and Technology*, **41** (1), 537–607.

Bort, J. (2014) Mark Zuckerberg Just Backtracked on Two of Facebook's Guiding Principles, But That's A Good Thing, *Business Insider*, 30 April, www.businessinsider.com/mark-zuckerberg-backtracks-on-principals-2014-4.

Box, G. E. P. and Draper, N. R. (1987) *Empirical Model-Building and Response Surfaces*, John Wiley & Sons.

Bradley, P. (2017) *Expert Internet Searching*, 5th edn, Facet Publishing.

Brett, M. R. (2012) Topic Modeling: a basic introduction, *Journal of Digital Humanities*, **2** (1), http://journalofdigitalhumanities.org/2-1/topic-modeling-a-basic-introduction-by-megan-r-brett.

Brin, S. and Page, L. (1998) The Anatomy of a Large-scale Hypertextual Web Search Engine, *Computer Networks and ISDN Systems*, **30** (1–7), 107–17.

Briscoe, G. and Mulligan, C. (2014) *Digital Innovation: the hackathon phenomenon*, www.creativeworkslondon.org.uk/wp-content/uploads/2013/11/Digital-Innovation-The-Hackathon-Phenomenon1.pdf.

British Library (2020) About Us: Transparency, https://www.bl.uk/about-us/freedom-of-information/transparency.

Brown, J. (2019) High-tech Ways to Keep Employees Happy, BBC News, 13 September, https://www.bbc.co.uk/news/business-49165358.

Brumfiel, G. (2011) Down the Petabyte Highway, *Nature*, **469** (7330), 20 January, 282–3.

Buckley Owen, T. (2017) *Successful Enquiry Answering Every Time: thinking your way from problem to solution*, Facet Publishing.

Burton, M. and Lyon, L. (2017) Data Science in Libraries, *Bulletin of the Association for Information Science and Technology*, 28 April, http://onlinelibrary.wiley.com/doi/10.1002/bul2.2017.1720430409/full.

Burton, M., Lyon, L., Erdmann, C. and Tijerina, B. (2018) *Shifting to Data Savvy: the future of data science in libraries*, Project Report, University of Pittsburgh, Pittsburgh, PA.

Buschman, J. (2003) *Dismantling the Public Sphere: situating and sustaining librarianship in the age of the new public philosophy*, Libraries Unlimited.

Byron, L. and Wattenberg, M. (2008) Stacked Graphs – Geometry & Aesthetics, *IEEE Transactions on Visualization and Computer Graphics*, **14** (6), 1245–52.

Cairo, A. (2016) *The Truthful Art: data, charts, and maps for communication*, New Riders, www.thefunctionalart.com.

Cass, S. (2017) The 2017 Top Programming Languages, https://spectrum. ieee.org/computing/software/the-2017-top-programming-languages.

Cellan-Jones, R. (2017) Disruption Is Over – and Facebook Won, BBC News, 14 August, https://www.bbc.co.uk/news/technology-40922041.

Christakis, N. A. and Fowler, J. H. (2009) *Connected: the amazing power of social networks and how they shape our lives*, Little Brown and Company.

CILIP (2018) Trustworthy Information Survey, SlideShare, Chartered Institute of Library and Information Professionals, 14 February, https://www.slideshare.net/CILIP/trustworthy-information-87989804.

Clarke, A. C. (1999) *Profiles of the Future: an inquiry into the limits of the possible*, Indigo.

Coleman, C. (2019) Police facial recognition surveillance court case starts, BBC News, 21 May, https://www.bbc.co.uk/news/uk-48315979.

Cooney, M. (2018) Cisco Predicts Nearly 5 Zettabytes of IP Traffic per Year by 2022, *Network World*, 28 November, https://www.networkworld.com/article/3323063/cisco-predicts-nearly-5-zettabytes-of-ip-traffic-per-year-by-2022.html.

Cox, A. (2018) Academic Librarianship as a Data Profession: the familiar and unfamiliar in the data role spectrum, CILIP, https://www.cilip.org.uk/members/group_content_view.asp?group= 201314&id=755941.

Crane, D. (1972) *Invisible Colleges: diffusion of knowledge in scientific communities*, University of Chicago Press.

Davenport, T. H. and Patil, D. J. (2012) Data Scientist: the sexiest job of the 21st century, *Harvard Business Review*, October, https://hbr.org/2012/10/data-scientist-the-sexiest-job-of-the-21st-century.

Demerjian, D. (2007) Rise of the Netflix Hackers, *Wired*, 15 March, https://www.wired.com/2007/03/rise-of-the-netflix-hackers.

Dent, S. (2018) Sony Unveils World's First 48-megapixel Smartphone Sensor, *Engadget*, 23 July, https://www.engadget.com/2018/07/23/sony-48-megapixel-smartphone-sensor.

Dinsmore, T. W. (2017) How GDPR Affects Data Science, KDnuggets, July, https://www.kdnuggets.com/2017/07/gdpr-affects-data-science.html.

Dodds, P. S., Muhamad, R. and Watts, D. J. (2003) An Experimental Study of Search in Global Social Networks, *Science*, **301** (5634), 827–9.

Donati, G. and Woolston, C. (2017) Information Management: data domination, *Nature*, **548** (7669), 613–14.

Duhigg, C. (2012) *The Power of Habit*, Random House.

Ekstrøm, J., Elbaek, M., Erdmann, C. and Grigorov, I. (2016) The Research Librarian of the Future: data scientist and co-investigator, LSE Impact Blog, 14 December, http://blogs.lse.ac.uk/impactofsocialsciences/2016/12/14/the-research-librarian-of-the-future-data-scientist-and-co-investigator/.

Etzkowitz, H. and Leydesdorff, L. (2000) The Dynamics of Innovation: from national systems and 'mode 2' to a triple helix of university-industry-government relations, *Research Policy*, **29** (2), 109–23.

Eysenbach, G. (2006) Infodemiology: tracking flu-related searches on the web for syndromic surveillance. In *AMIA Annual Symposium Proceedings*, **2006** (244), American Medical Informatics Association.

Fang, X. and Zhan, J. (2015) Sentiment Analysis Using Product Review Data, *Journal of Big Data*, **2**, https://journalofbigdata.springeropen.com/articles/10.1186/s40537-015-0015-2.

Federer, L. M., Lu, Y.-L. and Joubert, D. J. (2016) Data Literacy Training Needs of Biomedical Researchers, *Journal of the Medical Library Association*, **104** (1), 52–7.

Figuerola, C. G., Marco, F. J. G. and Pinto, M. (2017) Mapping the Evolution of Library and Information Science (1978–2014) Using Topic Modelling on LISA, *Scientometrics*, **112**, 1507–35.

Frické, M. (2009) The Knowledge Pyramid: a critique of the DIKW hierarchy, *Journal of Information Science*, **35** (2), 131–42.

Gaillard, M. and Pandolfi, S. (2017) CERN Data Centre Passes the 200-petabyte Milestone, https://cds.cern.ch/record/2276551.

Gallagher, J. (2019) NHS to Set Up National Artificial Intelligence Lab, BBC News, 8 August, https://www.bbc.co.uk/news/health-49270325.

Garfield, E. (2006) The History and Meaning of the Journal Impact Factor, *JAMA*, **295** (1), 90–3.

Gartner, R. (2016) *Metadata: shaping knowledge from antiquity to the semantic web*, Springer.

Gilbert, R., Lafferty, R., Hagger-Johnson, G., Harron, K., Zhang, L.-C., Smith, P., Dibben, C. and Goldstein, H. (2018) GUILD: guidance for information about linking data sets, *Journal of Public Health*, **40** (1), 191–8.

Ginsberg, J., Mohebbi, M. H., Patel, R. S., Brammer, L., Smolinkski, M. S. and Brilliant, L. (2009) Detecting Influenza Epidemics Using Search Engine Query Data, *Nature*, **457**, 1012–14.

GitHub (2019) External Resources, https://github.com/OpenRefine/OpenRefine/wiki/External-Resources.

Golder, S. A. and Macy, M. W. (2011) Diurnal and Seasonal Mood Vary with Work, Sleep, and Daylength Across Diverse Cultures, *Science*, **333** (6051), 30 September, 1878–81.

González-Ibáñez, R., Muresan, S. and Wacholder, N. (2011) Identifying Sarcasm in Twitter: a closer look. In *Proceedings of the 49th Annual Meeting of the Association for Computational Linguistics, Portland, Oregon, 19–24 June*, 581–6, https://pdfs.semanticscholar.org/55e3/6d6b45c91a0daa49234bd47b85647 0d6825c.pdf.

Guardian Data Blog (2014) University Research Excellence Framework 2014 – the full rankings, 18 December, https://www.theguardian.com/news/datablog/ng-interactive/2014/dec/18/university-research-excellence-framework-2014-full-rankings.

Gurstein, M. (2011) Open Data: empowering the empowered or effective data use for everyone?, *First Monday*, **16** (2–7), http://firstmonday.org/ojs/index.php/fm/article/viewArticle/3316/2764.

Hagen, L. (2018) Content Analysis of E-petitions with Topic Modelling: how to train and evaluate LDA models?, *Information Processing and Management*, **54**, 1292–307.

Haim, M., Graefe, A. and Brosius H-B. (2018) Burst of the Filter Bubble? Effects of personalization on the diversity of Google News, *Digital Journalism*, **6** (3), 6 July, https://www.tandfonline.com/doi/abs/10.1080/21670811.2017.1338145.

Hall, W. and Pesenti, J. (2017) *Growing the Artificial Intelligence Industry in the UK*, GOV.UK, 15 October, https://www.gov.uk/government/publications/growing-the-artificial-intelligence-industry-in-the-uk.

Harkness, T. (2016) *Big Data: does size matter?* Bloomsbury Sigma.

Harris, J. (2011) Word Clouds Considered Harmful, Nieman Lab, 13 October, https://www.niemanlab.org/2011/10/word-clouds-considered-harmful.

Hayashi, C. (1996) What is Data Science? Fundamental concepts and a heuristic example, *Data Science, Classification and Related Methods*, Springer, 40–51, https://link.springer.com/chapter/10.1007/978-4-431-65950-1_3.

Heath, T. (2009) Linked Data? Web of Data? Semantic Web? WTF?, blog, Tom Heath's Displacement Activities, 2 March, http://tomheath.com/blog/2009/03/linked-data-web-of-data-semantic-web-wtf/.

Heathman, A. (2018) Planning for a Life Without Death or Smartphones: what it's like to be a futurologist, *Evening Standard*, 26 July, https://www.standard.co.uk/tech/john-lewis-futurologist-john-vary-2030-a3895816.html.

Hilbert, M. (2015) A Review of Large-scale 'How Much Information?' Inventories: variations, achievements and challenges, *Information Research*, **20** (4), www.informationr.net/ir/20-4/paper688.html.

Himelboim, I., Golan, G., Moon, B. B. and Suto, R. J. (2014) A Social Networks Approach to Public Relations on Twitter: social mediators and mediated public relations, *Journal of Public Relations Research*, **26** (4), 359–79.

Hirsch, J. E. (2005) An Index to Quantify an Individual's Scientific Research Output, *Proceedings of the National Academy of Science of the United States of America*, **102** (46), 16569–72.

Hirschberg, J. and Manning, C. D. (2016) Advances in Natural Language Processing, *Science*, **349** (6245), 261–6.

House of Commons Science and Technology Committee (2018) *Algorithms in Decision-making: fourth report of session 2017–2019*, https://publications.parliament.uk/pa/cm201719/cmselect/cmsctech/351/351.pdf.

Hur, M., Kang, P. and Cho, S. (2016) Box-office Forecasting Based on Sentiments of Movie Reviews and Independent Subspace, *Information Sciences*, **372**, 608–24.

Hyndman, R. J. and Athanasopoulos, G. (2019) *Forecasting: principles and practice*, 3rd edn, OTexts, https://otexts.com/fpp3.

Idris, I. (2014) *Python Data Analysis*, Packt Publishing.

Information Commissioner's Office (2017) *Big Data, Artificial Intelligence, Machine Learning and Data Protection*, https://ico.org.uk/media/for-organisations/documents/2013559/big-data-ai-ml-and-data-protection.pdf.

Intellectual Property Office (2014) *Exceptions to Copyright: research*, October, https://assets.publishing.service.gov.uk/government/uploads/system/uploads/attachment_data/file/375954/Research.pdf.

Jänicke, S., Franzini, G., Cheema, M. F. and Scheuermann, G. (2015) On Close and Distant Reading in Digital Humanities: a survey and future challenges, paper given at Eurographics Conference on Visualization, 83–103, https://pdfs.semanticscholar.org/20cd/40f3f17dc7d8f49d368c2efbc2e27b0f2b33.pdf.

Jones, S., Ross, S. and Ruusalepp, R. (2009) *Data Audit Framework Methodology, draft for discussion, version 1.8*, Humanities Advanced Technology and Information Institute, Glasgow, https://data-audit.eu/DAF_Methodology.pdf.

Kalender, W. A. (2011) *Computed Tomography: fundamentals, system technology, image quality, applications*, 3rd edn, Wiley VCH.

Kaplan, A. (1964) *The Conduct of Inquiry: methodology for behavioral science*, Chandler Publishing.

Karalevicius, V., Degrande, N. and De Weerdt, J. (2018) Using Sentiment Analysis to Predict Interday Bitcoin Price Movements, *Journal of Risk Finance*, **19** (1), 56–75.

Karami, A. and Collins, M. (2019) What do the US West Coast Public Libraries Post on Twitter?, *Proceedings of the Association for Information Science and Technology*, **55** (1), 216–25, https://asistdl.onlinelibrary.wiley.com/doi/abs/10.1002/pra2.2018.14505501024.

Kay, D., Harrop, H., Chad, K., van Harmelen, M., Miller, P. and Pattern, D. (2010) *The JISC MOSAIC Project: Making Our Scholarly Activity Information Count – Final Report*, JISC, 8 April, http://repository.jisc.ac.uk/466.

Kelion, L. (2018) Facebook Seeks Facial Recognition Consent in EU and Canada, BBC News, 18 April, www.bbc.co.uk/news/technology-43797128.

Kerr, D. and Klonoff, D. C. (2019) Digital Diabetes Data and Artificial Intelligence: a time for humility not hubris, *Journal of Diabetes Science and Technology*, **13** (1), 123–7.

Kessler, M. M. (1963) Bibliographic Coupling Between Scientific Papers, *American Documentation*, **14** (1), 10–25.

Kitchin, R. (2014) *The Data Revolution: big data, open data, data infrastructures & their consequences*, Sage.

Kitchin, R. and McArdle, G. (2016) What Makes Big Data, Big Data? Exploring the ontological characteristics of 26 datasets, *Big Data & Society*, **3** (1), http://journals.sagepub.com/doi/abs/10.1177/2053951716631130.

Kleinberg, J. (2003) Bursty and Hierarchical Structure in Streams, *Data Mining and Knowledge Discovery*, **7** (4), 373–97.

Kleinfeld, J. (2002) Six Degrees: urban myth?, *Psychology Today*, 1 March, https://www.psychologytoday.com/gb/articles/200203/six-degrees-urban-myth.

Knapton, S. and Watson, L. (2017) Entire Human Chess Knowledge Learned and Surpassed by Deepmind's Alphazero in Four Hours, *Daily Telegraph*, 6 December, https://www.telegraph.co.uk/science/2017/12/06/entire-human-chess-knowledge-learned-surpassed-deepminds-alphazero.

Koltay, T. (2017) Data Literacy for Researchers and Data Librarians, *Journal of Librarianship and Information Science*, **49** (1), 3–14.

Kroski, E. (2017) *The Maker Space Librarian's Sourcebook*, Facet Publishing.

Kumar, R., Novak, J., Raghavan, P. and Tomkins, A. (2005) On the Bursty Evolution Blogspace, *World Wide Web*, 8 (2), 159–78.

Lamba, M. and Madhusudhan, M. (2018) Application of Sentiment Analysis in Libraries to Provide Temporal Information Services: a case study on various facets of productivity, *Social Network Analysis and Mining*, 8 (1), 1–12.

Laney, D. (2001) 3D Data Management: controlling data volume, velocity, and variety, blog, META Group, 6 February, https://blogs.gartner.com/doug-laney/files/2012/01/ad949-3D-Data-Management-Controlling-Data-Volume-Velocity-and-Variety.pdf.

Lange, A.-C., Lenglet, M. and Seyfert, R. (2016) Cultures of High-frequency Trading: mapping the landscape of algorithmic developments in contemporary financial markets, *Economy and Society*, **45** (2), 149–65.

Lanthaler, M. and Gütl, C. (2012) On Using JSON-LD to Create Evolvable RESTful Services, www.markus-lanthaler.com/research/on-using-json-ld-to-create-evolvable-restful-services.pdf.

Lazer, D., Kennedy, R., King, G. and Vespignani, A. (2014) The Parable of Google Flu: traps in big data analysis, *Science*, **343** (6176), 1203–5.

Leskovec, J. and Horvitz, E. (2008) Planetary-scale Views on a Large Instant Messaging Network, paper given at International World Wide Web Conference, 21–25 April 2008, Beijing, China, https://cs.stanford.edu/people/jure/pubs/msn-www08.pdf.

Lévis-Strauss, C. (1966) *The Savage Mind*, Oxford University Press.

Leydesdorff, L. and Nerghes, A. (2017) Co-word Maps and Topic Modeling: a comparison using small and medium-sized corpora (N<1000), *Journal of the Association for Information Science and Technology*, **68** (4), 1024–35.

Library of Congress (2008a) Dublin Core to MARC Crosswalk, https://www.loc.gov/marc/dccross.html.

Library of Congress (2008b) MARC to Dublin Core Crosswalk, https://www.loc.gov/marc/marc2dc.html.

Liu, B. (2015) *Sentiment Analysis: mining opinions, sentiments, and emotions*, Cambridge University Press.

Logan, E. and Shaw, W. (1987) An Investigation of the Co-author Graph, *Journal of the American Society for Information Science and Technology*, **38** (4), 262–8.

Lohr, S. (2012a) The Age of Big Data, *New York Times*, https://www.nytimes.com/2012/02/12/sunday-review/big-datas-impact-in-the-world.html.

Lohr, S. (2012b) How Big Data Became So Big, *New York Times*, www.nytimes.com/2012/08/12/business/how-big-data-became-so-big-unboxed.html.

Lunden, I. (2018) Google Goes All-In on Artificial Intelligence, Renames Research Division Google AI, *TechCrunch*, https://techcrunch.com/2018/05/08/google-goes-all-in-on-artificial-intelligence-renames-research-division-google-ai.

Mangalindan, J. P. (2012) Amazon's Recommendation Secret, *Fortune*, 30 July, http://fortune.com/2012/07/30/amazons-recommendation-secret/.

Mäntylä, M. V., Graziotin, D. and Kuutila, M. (2018) The Evolution of Sentiment Analysis – a review of research topics, venues, and top cited papers, *Computer Science Review*, **27**, 16–32.

Manyika, J., Chui, M., Brown, B., Bughin, J., Dobbs, R., Roxburgh, C. and Hung Byers, A. (2011) *Big Data: the next frontier for innovation, competition, and productivity*, www.mckinsey.com/business-functions/digital-mckinsey/our-insights/big-data-the-next-frontier-for-innovation.

Marr, B. (2015) *Big Data: using smart big data, analytics and metrics to make better decisions and improve performance*, John Wiley & Sons.

Marr, B. (2016) *Big Data for Small Business for Dummies*, John Wiley & Sons.

Marris, E. (2018) Animals Worldwide Stick Close to Home When Humans Move In, *Nature News*, 25 January, https://www.nature.com/articles/d41586-018-01240-w.

Martin, K. (2018) Ethical Implications and Accountability of Algorithms, *Journal of Business Ethics*, https://doi.org/10.1007/s10551-018-3921-3.

Matcher, E. (2016) Mapping Rio's Favelas, *Smithsonian*, 15 July, www.smithsonianmag.com/innovation/mapping-rios-favelas-180959816/.

Mathews, J. M. and Pardue, H. (2009) The Presence of IT Skills Sets in Librarian Position Announcements, *College & Research Libraries*, **70** (3), http://crl.acrl.org/index.php/crl/article/viewFile/16009/17455.

Mayer-Schönberger, V. and Cukier, K. (2013) *Big Data: a revolution that will transform how we live, work and think*, John Murray.

McCandless, D. (2012) *Information is Beautiful*, Collins, https://informationisbeautiful.net.

Merton, R. (1968) The Matthew Effect in Science, *Science*, **159** (3810), 56–63.

Messerli, F. H. (2012) Chocolate Consumption, Cognitive Function, and Nobel Laureates, *New England Journal of Medicine*, **367**, 1562–4.

Miles, I., Cassingena Harper, J., Georghiou, L., Keenan, M. and Popper, R. (2008) The Many Faces of Foresight. In Georghiou, L., Cassingena Harper, J., Keenan, M., Miles, I. and Popper, R. (eds), *The Handbook of Technology Foresight*, Edward Elgar.

Milgram, S. (1967) The Small World Problem, *Psychology Today*, **2** (1), 60–7.

Montjoye, Y.-A. de, Hildago, C. A., Verleysen, M. and Blondel, V. D. (2013) Unique in the Crowd: the privacy bounds of human mobility, *Scientific Reports*, **3** (1376), https://www.nature.com/articles/srep01376.

Moreno, J. L. (1978) *Who Shall Survive? Foundations of sociometry, group psychotherapy and sociodrama*, 3rd edn, Beacon House.

Moretti, F. (2013) *Distant Reading*, Verso Books.

Naisbitt, J. (1984) *Megatrends: ten new directions transforming our lives*, Grand Central Publishing.

Naughton, J. (2012a) Big Data: revolution by numbers, *Guardian*, 18 November, https://www.theguardian.com/technology/2012/nov/18/data-analysis-applied-business-science.

Naughton, J. (2012b) Why Big Data Is Now Such a Big Deal, *Guardian*, 18 March, https://www.theguardian.com/technology/2012/mar/18/big-data-storage-analysis-internet.

Newport, C. (2019) *Digital Minimalism: on living better with less technology*, Penguin.

Nicholson, S. (2006a) Approaching Librarianship from the Data: using biblio-mining for evidence-based librarianship, *Library Hi-Tech*, **24** (3), 369–75.

Nicholson, S. (2006b) Proof in the Pattern, *Library Journal (netconnect supplement)*, Winter, 2.

Nijman, V. and Nekaris, K. A-I. (2017) The Harry Potter Effect: the rise in trade of owls as pets in Java and Bali, Indonesia, *Global Ecology and Conservation*, **11**, 84–94.

NITRD (2016) *The Federal Big Data Research and Development Strategic Plan*, Big Data Senior Steering Group, Networking and Information Technology Research and Development Program, https://www.nitrd.gov/PUBS/bigdatardstrategicplan.pdf.

NMC (2017) *2017 Horizon Report*, Educause, New Media Consortium, 15 February, http://cdn.nmc.org/media/2017-nmc-horizon-report-library-EN.pdf.

Nurseitov, N., Paulson, M., Reynolds, R. and Izurieta, C. (2009) Comparison of JSON and XML Data Interchange Formats: a case study. In *Proceedings of the ISCA 22nd International Conference on Computer Applications in Industry and Engineering*, 157–62.

Nussbaumer Knaflic, C. (2015) *Storytelling with Data: a data visualization guide for business professionals*, John Wiley & Sons, www.storytellingwithdata.com.

OpenRefine (2018) 2018 Survey Results, http://openrefine.org/my%20category/2018/07/16/2018-survey-results.html.

O'Reilly, T. (2005) What is Web 2.0: Design Patterns and Business Models for the Next Generation of Software, O'Reilly, 30 September, https://www.oreilly.com/pub/a/web2/archive/what-is-web-20.html.

Pain, E. (2019) How to Keep a Lab Notebook, *Science*, 3 September, https://www.sciencemag.org/careers/2019/09/how-keep-lab-notebook.

Pariser, E. (2011) *The Filter Bubble: what the internet is hiding from you*, Penguin.

Partlo, K. (2010) The Pedagogical Data Reference Interview, *IASSIST Quarterly*, **33** (4), https://iassistquarterly.com/index.php/iassist/article/view/884.

Patil, D. (2015) A Memo to the American People from US Chief Data Scientist Dr DJ Patil, blog, https://obamawhitehouse.archives.gov/blog/2015/02/19/memo-american-people-us-chief-data-scientist-dr-dj-patil.

Payne, D. (2017) How Much Money Was Received in Payment of Library Fines per UK University During Academic Year 2015/16?, Figshare, 18 May, https://figshare.com/articles/League_table_of_UK_Universities_based_on_how_much_money_was_received_in_payment_of_library_fines_during_academic_year_2015_2016/4757989.

Pechenick, E. A., Danforth, C. M. and Dodds, P. S. (2015) Characterizing the Google Books Corpus: Strong limits to inferences of socio-cultural and linguistic evolution, *PloS ONE*, **10** (10), e0137041.

Perez, S. (2018) Facebook Rolls Out More API Restrictions and Shutdowns, Techcrunch, 2 July, https://techcrunch.com/2018/07/02/facebook-rolls-out-more-api-restrictions-and-shutdowns/.

Perkel, J. M. (2018) Why Jupyter is Data Scientists' Computational Notebook of Choice, *Nature*, 30 October, https://www.nature.com/articles/d41586-018-07196-1.

Pettit, M. (2016) Historical Time in the Age of Big Data: cultural psychology, historical change, and the Google Books Ngram Viewer, *History of Psychology*, **19** (2), 141–53.

PEW (2017) Most Americans – Especially Millennials – Say Libraries Can Help them Find Reliable, Trustworthy Information, 30 August, https://www.pewresearch.org/fact-tank/2017/08/30/most-americans-especially-millennials-say-libraries-can-help-them-find-reliable-trustworthy-information.

Piatetsky, G. (2017) New Leader, Trends, and Surprises in Analytics, Data Science, Machine Learning Software Poll, KDnuggets, https://www.kdnuggets.com/2017/05/poll-analytics-data-science-machine-learning-software-leaders.html.

Platt, E. L. (2019) *Network Science with Python and NetworkX Quick Start Guide*, Packt Publishing.

Pollack, J. and Adler, D. (2015) Emergent Trends and Passing Fads in Project Management Research: a scientometric analysis of changes in the field, *International Journal of Project Management*, **33** (1), 236–48.

Porta, S., Latora V., Wang, F., Rueda, S., Strano, E., Scellato, S., Cerdillo, A., Belli, E., Càrdenas, F., Cormenzana, B. and Latora, L. (2012) Street Centrality and the Location of Economic Activities in Barcelona, *Urban Studies*, **49** (7), 1471–88.

Prell, C. (2012) *Social Network Analysis*, Sage.

Press, G. (2016) Cleaning Big Data: most time-consuming, least enjoyable data science task, survey says, *Forbes*, 23 March, https://www.forbes.com/sites/gilpress/2016/03/23/data-preparation-most-time-consuming-least-enjoyable-data-science-task-survey-says/#16c74f616f63.

Priem, J., Taraborelli, D., Groth, P. and Neylon, C. (2010) Altmetrics: a manifesto, *Altmetrics*, 26 October, http://altmetrics.org/manifesto.

Pritchard, A. (1969) Statistical Bibliography or Bibliometrics?, *Journal of Documentation*, **25** (4), 348–9.

Provost, F. and Fawcett, T. (2013) *Data Science for Business: what you need to know about data mining and data-analytic thinking*, O'Reilly Media.

Rajan, A. (2017) Data is not the New Oil, BBC News, 9 October, www.bbc.co.uk/news/entertainment-arts-41559076.

Raju, J. (2017) Information Professional or IT Professional? The knowledge and skills required by academic librarians in the digital library environment, *Portal: Libraries and the Academy*, **17** (4), 739–57.

Ramírez Ortiz, M. G., Caballero Hoyos, J. R. and Ramírez López, M. G. (2004) The Social Networks of Academic Performance in a Student Context of Poverty in Mexico, *Social Networks*, **26** (2), 175–88.

Renaud, J., Britton, S., Wang, D. and Ogihara, M. (2015) Mining Library and University Data to Understand Library Use Patterns, *Electronic Library*, **33** (3), 355–72.

Reynolds, M. (2017) The Giant Piccadilly Billboard Is Going to Track Cars to Target Ads, *WIRED*, 10 October, www.wired.co.uk/article/piccadilly-circus-new-massive-advertising-screen.

Reznik-Zellen, R.C., Adamick, J. and McGinty, S. (2012) Tiers of Research Data Support Services, *Journal of eScience Librarianship*, **1** (1), Article 5.

Rhody, L. M. (2012) Topic Model Data for Topic Modeling and Figurative Language, *Journal of Digital Humanities*, **2** (1), http://journalofdigitalhumanities.org/2-1/topic-model-data-for-topic-modeling-and-figurative-language-by-lisa-m-rhody.

Rice, R. and Southall, J. (2017) Top Tips for a Data Reference Interview, CILIP blog, 13 February, https://archive.cilip.org.uk/blog/top-tips-data-reference-interview.

Richards, D. R. (2013) The Content of Historical Books as an Indicator of Past Interest in Environmental Issues, *Biodiversity and Conservation*, **22** (12), 2795–803.

Rosenbaum, M. (2015) 10 Things We Found Out Because of Freedom of Information, BBC News, 2 January, https://www.bbc.co.uk/news/magazine-30645383.

Rosenthal, D. S. H. (2017) The Medium-term Prospects for Long-term Storage Systems, *Library Hi Tech*, **35** (1), 11–31.

Rowley, J. (2007) The Wisdom Hierarchy: representation of the DIKW hierarchy, *Journal of Information Science*, **33** (2), 163–80.

Sagiroglu, S. and Sinanc, D. (2013) Big Data: a review. In *Proceedings of the International Conference on Collaboration Technologies and Systems*, Institute of Electrical and Electronics Engineers, 42–7, http://ieeexplore.ieee.org/abstract/document/6567202/.

Schelling, T. C. (2006) *Micromotives and Macrobehaviour*, W. W. Norton & Company.

Sclater, N. and Mullan, J. (2017) *Learning Analytics and Student Success: assessing the evidence*, Jisc briefing, http://repository.jisc.ac.uk/6560/1/learning-analytics_and_student_success.pdf.

Secker, J., Morrison, C., Stewart, N. and Horton, L. (2016) To Boldly Go . . . the librarian's role in text and data mining, blog, CILIP, 19 September, https://archive.cilip.org.uk/blog/boldly-go-librarians-role-text-data-mining.

Sekinah, T. (2019) Data is Not the New Oil Say Prof Sir Nigel Shadbolt and Sir Tim Berners-Lee, DataIQ, 14 November, https://www.dataiq.co.uk/articles/articles/data-is-not-the-new-oil-say-prof-sir-nigel-shadbolt-and-sir-tim-berners-lee.

Semeler, A. R., Pinto, A. L. and Rozandos, H. B. F. (2017) Data Science in Data Librarianship: core competencies of a data librarian, *Journal of Librarianship and Information Science*, **51** (3), 771–80.

Serrano-Guerrero, J., Olivas, J. A., Romero, F. P. and Herrera-Viedma, E. (2015) Sentiment Analysis: a review and comparative analysis of web services, *Information Sciences*, **311**, 18–38.

Shultes, A. (2019) 'Racist' AI Art Warns Against Bad Training Data, BBC News, 17 September, https://www.bbc.co.uk/news/technology-49726652.

Si, L., Xing, W., Zhuang, X., Hua, X. and Zhou, L. (2015) Investigation and Analysis of Research Data Services in University Libraries, *Electronic Library*, **33** (3), 417–49.

Siguenza-Guzman, L., Saquicela, V., Avila-Ordóñez, E., Vandewalle, J. and Cattrysse, D. (2015) Literature Review of Data Mining Applications in Academic Libraries, *Journal of Academic Librarianship*, **41** (4), 499–510.

Silge, J. and Robinson, D. (2017) *Text Mining with R: a tidy approach*, O'Reilly Media, www.tidytextmining.com.

Silver, N. (2012) *The Signal and the Noise*, Penguin.

Small, H. (1973) Co-citation in the Scientific Literature: a new measure of the relationship between two documents, *Journal of the American Society for Information Science*, **24** (4), 265–9.

Sporny, M. (2014) JSON-LD and Why I Hate the Semantic Web, blog, 21 January, https://web.archive.org/web/20180501193640/ http://manu.sporny.org/2014/json-ld-origins-2/.

Springboard (2016) The Data Science Process, KDnuggets, March, https://www.kdnuggets.com/2016/03/data-science-process.html.

Stephens-Davidowitz, S. (2018) *Everybody Lies: what the internet can tell us about who we really are*, Bloomsbury.

Stewart, B. and Walker, J. (2018) Build It and They Will Come? Patron engagement via Twitter at historically black college and university libraries, *Journal of Academic Librarianship*, **44**, 118–24.

Stuart, D. (2011) *Facilitating Access to the Web of Data: a guide for librarians*, Facet Publishing.

Stuart, D. (2014) *Web Metrics for Library and Information Professionals*, Facet Publishing.

Stuart, D. (2016) *Practical Ontologies for Informational Professionals*, Facet Publishing.

Stuart, D. (2018) Open Bibliometrics and Undiscovered Public Knowledge, *Online Information Review*, **42** (3), 412–18.

Stuart, D., Baynes, G., Hrynaszkiewicz, I., Allin, K., Penny, D., Lucraft, M. and Astell, M. (2018) Practical Challenges for Researchers in Data Sharing, *Springer Nature*, 27 March, https://researchdata.springernature.com/users/69154-springer-nature/posts/31633-whitepaper-practical-challenges-for-researchers-in-data -sharing.

Sugimoto, C. R., Li, D., Russell, T. G., Finlay, S. C. and Ding, Y. (2011) The Shifting Sands of Disciplinary Development: analyzing North American library and information science dissertations using latent Dirichlet allocation, *Journal of the American Society for Information Science and Technology*, **62** (1), 185–204.

Swan, A. and Brown, S. (2008) *The Skills, Role and Career Structure of Data Scientists and Curators: an assessment of current practice and future needs*, report to the JISC, https://eprints.soton.ac.uk/266675/.

Swanson, D. R. (1986) Undiscovered Public Knowledge, *Library Quarterly*, **56** (2), 103–18.

Tancer, B. (2009) *Click: what we do online and why it matters*, Harper Collins.

Taylor, D. (2016) Battle of the Data Science Venn Diagrams, KDnuggets, 36. www.kdnuggets.com/2016/10/battle-data-science-venn-diagrams.html.

Tenopir, C., Hughes, D., Allard, S., Frame, M., Birch, B., Baird, L., Sandusky, R., Langseth, M. and Lundeen, A. (2015) Research Data Services in Academic Libraries: data intensive roles for the future?, *Journal of eScience Librarianship*, **4** (2), art 4, 1–21.

Tenopir, C., Talja, S., Horstmann, W., Late, E., Hughes, D., Pollock, D., Schmidt, B., Baird, L., Sandusky, R. J. and Allard, S. (2017) Research Data Services in European Academic Research Libraries, *LIBER Quarterly*, **27** (1), 24–44.

Thelwall, M., Wouters, P. and Fry, J. (2008) Information-centred Research for Large-scale Analyses of New Information Sources, *Journal of the American Society for Information Science and Technology*, **59** (9), 1523–7 (see also cybermetrics.wlv.ac.uk/icr.html).

Twenge, J. M., Campbell, W. K. and Gentile, B. (2012) Increase in Individualistic Words and Phrases in American Books, 1960–2008, *Plos ONE*, https://journals.plos.org/plosone/article?id=10.1371/journal.pone.0040181.

Twenge, J. M., Campbell, W. K. and Gentile, B. (2013) Changes in Pronoun Use in American Books and the Rise of Individualism, 1960–2008, *Journal of Cross-Cultural Psychology*, **44** (3), 406–15.

Valdivia, A., Luzón, M. V. and Herrera, F. (2017) Sentiment Analysis in TripAdvisor, *IEEE Intelligent Systems*, **32** (4), 72–7.

VanderPlas, J. (2016) *Python Data Science Handbook*, O'Reilly Media, https://jakevdp.github.io/PythonDataScienceHandbook.

van Hooland, S. and Verborgh, R. (2014) *Linked Data for Libraries, Archives, and Museums: how to clean, link and publish your metadata*, Facet Publishing.

Venturini, T., Munk, A. and Meunier, A. (2018) Data-Sprint: a Public Approach to Digital Research. In Lury, C., Clough, P., Michael, M., Fensham, R., Lammes, S., Last, A. and Uprichard, E. (eds), *Routledge Handbook of Interdisciplinary Research Methods*, Routledge.

Vryzakis, A., Scott, A. and Foulds, H. (2018) Open Data Day: seven weird and wonderful open datasets, Open Data Institute, 2 March, https://theodi.org/article/the-open-data-olympics-seven-weird-and-wonderful-open-datasets/.

Wakefield, J. (2019) Dangerous AI Offers to Write Fake News, BBC News, 27 August, https://www.bbc.co.uk/news/technology-49446729.

Waldrop, M. M. (2013) Massive Open Online Courses, aka MOOCs, Transform Higher Education and Science, *Nature Magazine*, 13 March, https://www.scientificamerican.com/article/massive-open-online-courses-transform-higher-education-and-science/.

Waltman, L. (2017) Large-scale Visualization of Science: methods, tools, and applications, presented at the International workshop on data-driven science mapping, 3 June, Yonsei University, Seoul, Korea, https://www.slideshare.net/LudoWaltman/largescale-visualization-of-science-methods-tools-and-applications.

Waltman, L. (2018) Responsible Visualization, tweet, 13 April, https://twitter.com/LudoWaltman/status/984901539746660352.

WEF (2012) *Big Data, Big Impact: new possibilities for international development*, World Economic Forum, 22 January, http://www3.weforum.org/docs/WEF_TC_MFS_BigDataBigImpact_Briefing_2012.pdf.

Wells, H. G. (1932) Wanted: professors of foresight!, *Futures Research Quarterly*, **3** (1), 89–91, http://foresightinternational.com.au/wp-content/uploads/2015/09/Wells_Wanted_Profs_of_Fsight_1932.pdf.

Weng, J. and Lee, B-S. (2011) Event Detection on Twitter, *Fifth International AAAI Conference on Weblogs and Social Media*, https://www.aaai.org/ocs/index.php/ICWSM/ICWSM11/paper/viewPaper/2767.

Wickham, H. and Grolemund, G. (2016) *R for Data Science*, O'Reilly Media, https://r4ds.had.co.nz.

WLCG (2018) Worldwide LHC Computing Grid: about, http://wlcg-public.web.cern.ch/about.

Wong, J. C. (2019) Facebook's Zuckerberg Announces Privacy Overhaul: 'We don't have the strongest reputation', *Guardian*, 30 April, https://www.theguardian.com/technology/2019/apr/30/facebook-f8-conference-privacy-mark-zuckerberg.

Xia, J. and Wang, M. (2014) Competencies and Responsibilities of Social Science Data Librarians: an analysis of job descriptions, *College & Research Libraries*, **75** (3), 362–88.

Xie, S., Wang, G., Lin, S. and Yu, P. S. (2012) Review Spam Detection Via Temporal Pattern Discovery, *KDD '12: Proceeding of the 18th ACM SIGKDD International Conference on Knowledge Discovery and Data Mining*, https://dl.acm.org/citation.cfm?id=2339662.

Yan, E. and Ding, Y. (2009) Applying Centrality Measures to Impact Analysis: a coauthorship network analysis, *Journal of the American Society for Information Science and Technology*, **60** (10), 2107–18.

Yelton, A. (2019) HAMLET: neural-net-powered prototypes for library discovery, *Library Technology Reports*, **55** (1), 10–15, https://journals.ala.org/index.php/ltr/issue/view/709.

Zang, S., Ding, M., Smith, D., Tyler, P., Rakotoarivelo, T. and Kaafar, M. A (2019) The Impact of Adverse Weather Conditions on Autonomous Vehicles: how rain, snow, fog and hail affect the performance of a self-driving car, *IEEE Vehicular Technology Magazine*, **14** (2), 103–11.

Zhang, L., Wang, S. and Liu, B. (2018) Deep Learning for Sentiment Analysis: a survey, *WIREs: Data Mining and Knowledge Discovery*, 8 (4), e1253.

Zins, C. (2007) Conceptual Approaches for Defining Data, Information, and Knowledge, *Journal of the American Society for Information Science and Technology*, **58** (4), 479–93.

Zwaard, K. (2017) Announcing the Library of Congress Congressional Data Challenge, The Signal, blog, 19 October, https://blogs.loc.gov/thesignal/2017/10/congressional-data-challenge.

Appendix – Programming concepts for data science

The aim of this book is not to introduce programming, but rather to introduce data science in a way that shows that it is not difficult to move away from pre-packaged desktop software and start integrating some programming in your own analyses. This appendix includes more detail on some of the programming concepts used throughout this book, and is designed to try and help absolute beginners look more closely at the code rather than gloss over the code they come across in the book.

Like the book as a whole, the appendix is based on the idea that there is a lot that can be achieved with very little code. It is structured according to the main things you need to know to make sense of the programming in this book:

- variables, data types
- importing libraries
- functions and methods
- loops and conditionals.

Each concept is illustrated with examples from Python and R. They are not designed to be comprehensive introductions to the concepts, but rather practical introductions reflecting how they are used within the examples in this book. In the same way that similar ideas can be expressed in different ways in the same language, so it is with programming. When you start programming you will inevitably focus on writing code that works, as you progress however you will want to start writing code that is also efficient and maybe, eventually, aesthetically pleasing.

These examples are available in two notebooks on GitHub, one for the Python examples and one for the R examples: https://github.com/dpstuart/jupyter/blob/master/Chapter_AppendixPython.ipynb and https://github.com/dpstuart/jupyter/blob/master/Chapter_AppendixR.ipynb.

Variables, data types and other classes

Programming is about the manipulation of objects represented in a computer's memory. These objects can consist of the inbuilt data types, and newly defined classes of object. The basic data types (e.g. strings, integers and real numbers) are similar across high level languages, however more complex classes of object may be specific to a particular language. A variable's data type also determines which functions or methods can be applied to it.

Within this book various more complex data types are used, including dictionaries (unordered collection of key-value pairs), data frames (tables of heterogeneous data), and corpora (a collection of text objects). Some data types are already built into a language (e.g. strings and integers), some need to be imported (corpora), and some exist in some languages but need to be imported in others (e.g. data frames).

In neither Python nor R is it necessary to declare the variables, or the type of variable that you are using. It is simply a case of assigning the value to a particular variable (Box A.1). The process is similar whether you are assigning a snippet of text or one of the more complex object types, although for more complex object types it is generally carried out by assigning the result of a function rather than explicitly stating the value in the code. For example, we might state that we want to assign the last 100 tweets with a particular hashtag to a variable, we don't actually state what the values of those 100 tweets are.

Box A.1 Assigning a string and an integer to variables in Python and R

Python

Assigning a string and an integer to variables in Python:

```
name='David'
age=44
print(name, age)
>>> David 44
```

It can often be useful to be able to explore the type of variables with the type() function:

```
type(name)
>>> str
```

R

Assignment in R can be done with an =, but for historical reasons is generally done with <-. The c() function is used to combine the results.

```
name<- 'David'
age<-44
print (c(name, age))
>>> 'David' '44'

typeof(name)
>>> 'character'
```

Import libraries

Importing libraries allows us to stand on the shoulders of the programming giants who have come before. One of the reasons that we can do so much with relatively little code is that others have already written much of the code we need, and we can download this code to our computers and import it to our programs as and when it is required.

Within this book all the examples include the requisite import statements, unfortunately this is not always the case. While Stack Overflow (https://stackoverflow.com) is undoubtedly one of the most useful websites for programmers, too often there is the presumption that the import statements are unnecessary as readers know which libraries are being used. This can be extremely frustrating to beginners and more established programmers.

Importing libraries is actually a two-step process, as before a library can be imported it must actually be installed. The installation process may depend on the programming language, the integrated development environment that you are using, and whether the library is part of the language's standard library, indexed in the main repository of libraries, or merely sitting on an obscure website. Box A.2 explains how to import the 'time' library in Python and packages in the Comprehensive R Archive Network (CRAN) repository in R.

Box A.2 How to install libraries and packages
Python
The 'time' library is part of the Python Standard Library (https://docs.python.org/3/library), and, as would be expected, includes many time related functions. The 'sleep' function suspends the code that is being executed for a length of time in seconds, which may be useful if you wish to slow the rate of requests you send to a web server.

The whole module may be imported and functions referred to via the module:

```
import time as t
t.sleep(5)
```

The whole module may be imported and functions referred to directly:

```
from time import *
sleep(5)
```

Just the functions that are required may be imported:

```
from time import sleep
sleep(5)
```

R

In R installing packages that are in the CRAN repository is typically very simple:

```
install.packages('leaflet')
```

Once they have been installed it is equally simple to use them:

```
library(leaflet)
```

For example, the leaflet library means it is very simple to add an OpenStreetMap to a notebook:

```
m <- leaflet()
m <- addTiles(m)
m <- addMarkers(m, lng=-1.8281187, lat=52.6834463,
                   popup="Samuel Johnson's Birthplace")
m
```

Potential conflicts between functions with the same name in different libraries may be resolved with double colons between the package name and a function name. For example:

```
m <- leaflet::addTiles(m)
```

Functions and methods

It is not necessary for programming beginners to get overly concerned about the difference between methods and functions (or indeed, depending on the programming language, whether there is such a difference). It is sufficient to know that there are named sections of code that can be called and run from elsewhere.

These functions and methods are how we manipulate the variables and other classes, and build on other people's code. You can define your own functions, as explained in Box A.3, although in this book we have simply used the functions and methods in other people's functions, passing parameters as necessary.

Where lines of code are complicated and difficult to understand, it is often because multiple functions are being used, with the results of one function being passed as a parameter to another. When nesting functions, the biggest challenge for beginners is often making sure you get your brackets in the right place. Although integrated development environments may help by colour-coding brackets, it can nonetheless still be difficult to get brackets in the right place.

Box A.3 Building a function in Python and R
Python

In Python a function built with a **def** statement is followed by the name of the function, and a list of the parameters. This is followed by the commands to carry out, and what to return if necessary.

The following function simply adds the squares of two numbers, and then returns the result to where it was called from:

```
def squareTwoNumbers(x,y):
    z=x**2 + y**2
    return z
```

Once a function has been defined, it can be called as necessary with the appropriate parameters:

```
squareTwoNumbers(3, 4)
>>> 25
```

Predefined functions can be called in a similar fashion, for example the **len()** function returns the length of a string:

```
len ('hello world')
>>> 11
```

Methods are like functions, but act on the object. String methods can be particularly important in data cleaning:

```
a=' hEILo wORLD'
a.strip()
>>>'hEILo wORLD'
a.lower()
>>>' hello world'
```

R

Similarly in R:

```
squareTwoNumbers <- function(x,y){
    x^2+y^2
    }

squareTwoNumbers(3,4)
>>>25
```

Again many inbuilt functions may be called, for example returning the length of the string:

```
nchar('hello world')
>>> 11
```

But it is always worth being aware that there may be better – or at least more appropriate – functions for doing what you want in another library.

Loops and conditionals

The two other most important features of programming to be aware of are loops and conditionals. A loop is how you get a computer to repeat a set of instructions multiple times without actually repeating the instructions multiple times. As has already been mentioned, the objective may be achieved in code in multiple different ways, and loops are a good example of this. For example, a loop may be achieved in Python with either a *for* loop or a *while* loop. As only *for* loops are used in examples in this book, only *for* examples are given below.

Conditionals are used to tell a computer to only do things under certain conditions. For example, if it is raining take an umbrella. Typically conditionals use variations of **if**, **else** and specific logical operators (these may be expressed differently in the different languages). As well as the if and else, Python has an elif and R has elseif, which are similar to else, but you can have more than one of them. Table A.1 lists the most common logical operators used in Python and R, and Box A.4 explains the for loop in Python and R.

Table A.1 *Logical operators for some conditions in Python and R*

Condition	Python and R operator
Equals	==
Not equals	!=
Less than	<
Less than or equal to	<=
Greater than	>
Greater than or equal to	>=

Box A.4 The for loop in Python and R

Python

In the for loop example below, x iterates over the numbers in the range 1 to 10. If the number is not equal to 7, it displays the number on the screen, otherwise (when it equals 7) it displays 'Lucky 7!':

```
for x in range(1, 10):
    if x !=7:
        print (x)
    else:
        print ("Lucky 7!")
```

R

A similar loop in R would be as follows:

```
for(i in 1:10) {
    if (i != 7){print (i)}
    else {print ("Lucky 7!")}
}
```

Final words of advice

Programming for data science is not rocket science (unless you happen to be doing data science for NASA), and while programming can make it very simple to carry out large-scale complex analysis with just a few lines of code, you may just as easily find yourself totally stumped because the program is not doing what you want, or indeed anything at all!

Although computers are very useful tools, they are nonetheless tools. Totally dumb, so your programming must be precise and accurate. An errant bracket, a disjointed indentation, a mistyped variable name or simply trying to parse the wrong data type to a function can quickly bring your program grinding to a halt. This doesn't mean programming is beyond you, merely that you may have to spend some time going through your code, line by line, possibly character by character, trying to find out exactly where it has gone wrong. You will find many idiosyncrasies between the different languages. For example, anyone looking closely at the outputs of the two range functions above will notice they work slightly differently, with Python 'stopping short', and never printing 10.

Further reading

There are numerous programming books and courses available, and it is important to focus on what you need to know rather than trying to learn everything about a language or scurrying down the avenue of what looks most interesting (e.g. programming mobile apps). While many of the books are freely available online, or as e-books from libraries, I also recommend using hard copies of the books that you are going to return to most often. You will undoubtedly benefit from the browsability of a physical copy on your desk rather than constantly swapping between windows on your desktop.

O'Reilly publishes several books on programming, including some specifically for data science and particular aspects of data science:

- VanderPlas, J. (2016) *Python Data Science Handbook*, O'Reilly Media, https://jakevdp.github.io/PythonDataScienceHandbook
- Wickham, H. and G. Grolemund (2016) *R for Data Science*, O'Reilly Media, https://r4ds.had.co.nz
- Silge, J. and D. Robinson (2017) *Text Mining with R: a tidy approach*, O'Reilly Media, www.tidytextmining.com

And these two are also recommended:

- Hyndman, R. J. and G. Athanasopoulos (2019) *Forecasting: principles and practice*, 3rd edn, OTexts, https://otexts.com/fpp3; provides a comprehensive introduction to forecasting with R
- Platt, E. L. (2019) *Network Science with Python and NetworkX Quick Start Guide*, Packt Publishing.

Index